From Death...

...to Life

A Biblical Guide to True Salvation

John A. Woolwine

Printed in the United States of America

Second Edition

Published by Woolwine Publishing

This expanded edition incorporates and builds upon the material of the first edition, integrating study and reflection material for deeper engagement.

DEDICATION

To my beloved wife, Edna—
my closest companion, my encourager, and my faithful friend. Your patience, love, and steadfast devotion have been a living testimony of God's grace to me. Thank you for walking beside me through every season of life, praying for me, and standing firm when God was shaping my heart and calling.

To our children—Patrick, Janell, and Michele—and to your husbands, wives, and precious families:
You are each a gift from the Lord. My deepest prayer is that you will know, love, and follow Jesus Christ with all your heart, soul, mind, and strength, and that your lives would bear fruit for His glory.

To my grandchildren and to your families:
Each one of you is deeply loved, prayed for, and entrusted to the Lord. May He draw you to Himself, guard you in His truth, and make you steadfast in faith for generations to come.

And to the pastors, teachers, and mentors God used to guide, correct, encourage, and equip me—
those who faithfully taught the Word, modeled obedience, spoke truth when it was needed, and trusted me with the responsibility to teach and lead:
Thank you. This study guide is written in gratitude for your faithfulness and in recognition that God often shapes His servants through the care and confidence of others.

This study guide is dedicated to all of you—with a heart full of gratitude and a prayerful hope that God would use these pages to strengthen faith, grant assurance, and draw many from death to life in Christ.

May the Lord bless you and keep you, and may Christ be your greatest treasure.

TABLE OF CONTENTS

TABLE OF CONTENTS

PREFACE

From Death to Life:

A Biblical Guide to True Salvation

Salvation is the most important reality any human being will ever face. Nothing matters more—because nothing reaches deeper into our present lives or stretches farther into our eternal future. Yet in an age of confusion, distraction, religious pluralism, and shallow spiritual messages, few questions are more misunderstood than this one:

What does it mean to be truly saved?

For many, salvation has been reduced to a fleeting emotional experience, a recited prayer, a childhood memory, or a vague hope that "God will understand." Others treat it as a moral improvement plan or a reward for sincerity. Still others assume they are Christians simply because they grew up in church or live in a religious culture. But Scripture speaks with unmistakable clarity:

Eternal life is found only in Jesus Christ—
on His terms—
revealed in His Word,
accomplished by His grace,
and applied by His Spirit.

This book exists to help believers and seekers alike slow down, open the Scriptures, and examine what God Himself says about salvation. Not a diluted message. Not a modernized message. But the biblical gospel—the message Jesus proclaimed, the apostles defended, and the church has treasured for generations.

A Need for Clarity and Assurance

We live in a time when many profess Christ yet struggle with assurance, joy, or spiritual fruit. Some have never been taught what salvation actually is. Others have been shaped by messages of cheap grace—salvation without repentance, faith without surrender, forgiveness without transformation.

This book is written with a pastoral burden: to bring clarity where confusion exists, and assurance where doubt has taken root—not by pointing readers inward, but by directing them again and again to the saving work of God in Christ.

How This Book Is Designed

From Death to Life is intentionally structured to follow the unfolding logic of Scripture. Each chapter builds upon the last, forming a coherent, gospel-centered journey through the doctrine and experience of salvation:

- Who God is
- Who we are and why we need salvation
- What Christ accomplished
- How the Holy Spirit applies redemption
- What new life in Christ looks like
- How believers persevere and finish with hope

This book is meant to be used **thoughtfully and prayerfully**, whether individually, in families, or in group settings. Each section includes Scripture, doctrinal teaching, and reflection questions designed not merely to inform the mind, but to engage the heart and shape the life.

This is not a workbook of opinions, nor a theological debate manual. It is a guided walk through God's Word—meant to lead participants to worship, conviction, assurance, and obedience.

A Word About Scripture

Scripture is the foundation of every session.
God's Word—not human experience, tradition, or feeling—defines salvation, shapes faith, and anchors assurance.

While human emotions fluctuate, the Word of God remains unchanging. This study guide stands unapologetically upon that Word.

Who This Book Is For

This book is written for:

- Those honestly seeking to understand the gospel
- Believers desiring deeper assurance and clarity
- Parents and teachers discipling others in foundational truth
- Small groups and churches studying salvation together
- Anyone who wants to understand what it means to pass from death to life

Whether you have been walking with Christ for many years or are beginning to ask eternal questions, this study is designed to meet you where you are—and point you to the Savior who gives life.

A Prayerful Invitation

My prayer is simple:

As you work through these chapters, you will encounter
the God who saves,
the Christ who died and rose again,
and the Spirit who gives life.

I pray you will:

- marvel at God's holiness,
- feel the seriousness of sin,
- rejoice in the sufficiency of Christ,
- grow in assurance rooted in grace,
- and walk confidently in the love of the Father.

If you are already a believer, may this book strengthen your faith and deepen your assurance.

If you are not yet a believer, may God use His Word to awaken your heart and draw you to Christ.

The gospel is not merely information—it is an invitation.

"For everyone who calls on the name of the Lord will be saved."
—Romans 10:13

May God use these pages to bring many from death to life.
To Him alone be all the glory.

INTRODUCTION

From Death to Life:

A Biblical Invitation Rooted in Lived Experience

The aim of this book is not to promote a theological system or defend a tradition, but to present the teaching of Scripture as clearly, faithfully, and pastorally as possible. The Bible itself is the foundation of everything explored in these sessions. Doctrinal conclusions are drawn not from allegiance to any movement or name, but from the consistent testimony of the Word of God.

Where theological language is used, it serves only to clarify and summarize what Scripture teaches—not to replace or overshadow it. The goal throughout this book is not to lead participants toward a system, but toward Christ Himself, as He is revealed in the Scriptures.

A Personal Word of Context

Although this book is designed for group discussion and biblical exploration, it does not emerge from abstraction. It is shaped by lived experience—by the reality that one can be deeply involved in church life and still be spiritually dead.

For many years, I believed I was saved. I knew Christian language, participated actively in church, taught classes, and even preached on occasion. From the outside, my life appeared committed and faithful.

But beneath that appearance was a divided heart. Sin was not merely an occasional struggle—it was a pattern. Though I professed Christ, I lived for myself. I had religion, but not redemption. Knowledge, but not new life.

Through that season, God was not silent. The Holy Spirit confronted my false assurance, exposed my self-deception, and pressed upon me the truth that salvation is not measured by activity, sincerity, or familiarity with church—but by union with Christ.

That season ended not with self-reform, but with surrender. Not perfectly, but genuinely. God did not make me religious—He made me alive. What Scripture calls new birth, I came to know personally. That transformation is not the focus of this study, but it is the soil from which it grew.

Why This Book Exists

This book is written for those who may:

- assume they are saved because of church involvement or religious familiarity,
- struggle with assurance and do not understand why,
- feel conviction without clarity,
- long to understand what salvation truly is and how it changes a life.

It is also written for believers who desire to ground their faith more firmly in Scripture—to understand not only that they are saved, but what God has done, how He saves, and why assurance rests in Him alone.

Most of all, this study exists to keep the focus where Scripture keeps it:
not on our performance, but on God's grace;
not on our effort, but on Christ's finished work;
not on religious identity, but on new life.

A Shared Journey Through Scripture

This book is meant to be worked through slowly and prayerfully. Each session builds upon the last, inviting participants to listen carefully to God's Word, reflect honestly, and respond humbly.

The goal is not to produce experts, but disciples.
Not merely informed minds, but awakened hearts.
Not temporary emotion, but lasting faith and assurance.

If God could take a man who lived with confidence in religion yet bondage to sin and bring him from death to life, He can do the same for anyone who comes to Christ in repentance and faith. That is not my story alone—it is the promise of the gospel.

May God use this book to awaken hearts, strengthen faith, grant true assurance, and draw many into the joy of knowing Jesus Christ.

To Him be all the glory.

CHAPTER 1

God Is Sovereign and Holy
The Foundation of All Theology

Chapter Overview

Every discussion of salvation must begin with God. Before we ask what it means to be saved, we must first ask who God is. If our understanding of God is distorted, shallow, or man-centered, our understanding of salvation will be equally flawed. Scripture never begins with humanity's needs or abilities—it begins with God's nature and His eternal majesty.[1]

This chapter lays the foundation for everything that follows by examining God's character as He has revealed Himself in His Word.

This book will help you see why:

- Salvation must begin with God, not humanity
- God's sovereignty rules over all things
- God's holiness exposes the seriousness of sin
- God's righteousness and justice demand judgment
- God is Triune—Father, Son, and Holy Spirit—working together to save

> "In the beginning, God created the heavens and the earth."
> —Genesis 1:1

The Bible opens not with an argument for God's existence, but with a declaration of His supremacy. God does not arise from the creation; creation arises from God. He is uncreated, eternal, self-existent, and absolute in His being. All that exists, all of creation, derives meaning, order, and purpose from Him.

Section 1 — Why We Must Begin With God

Before Scripture explains salvation, it reveals the God who saves. Scripture never begins with humanity's potential, goodness, or ability. It begins with the Creator—eternal, sovereign, holy, and self-existent.

God does not exist to serve human purposes. Humanity exists to glorify God. When salvation is framed around human experience rather than God's character, it becomes distorted. Grace is minimized. Sin is softened. God becomes small, and salvation becomes shallow. Scripture insists that salvation flows **from God**, **by God**, and **for God**.[1]

Beginning with God reminds us that:

- Salvation is God's idea, not humanity's invention.
- God defines the problem of sin and the solution of grace.
- God sets the terms by which sinners are saved.

This is why theology always begins with God. Everything else—sin, grace, redemption, faith—only makes sense when God is rightly known.

Reflection and Discussion

1. Why do you think people are often tempted to begin discussions about salvation with themselves rather than with God?
2. How does beginning with God change the way you think about salvation?
3. In what ways can a man-centered view of salvation distort the gospel?

Section 2 - God Is Sovereign Over All Things

To say that God is sovereign means that He reigns supreme over all creation. Nothing exists independently of His will. Nothing occurs outside His authority. Nothing can frustrate or overturn His purposes.[2]

> "Our God is in the heavens; He does all that He pleases."
> —Psalm 115:3

God is not reacting to history—He is directing it. Scripture presents Him as the One who creates, sustains, governs, and fulfills all things according to His wise and holy purposes. Scripture affirms that God:

- creates according to His will (Genesis 1:1)
- rules over nations and history (Daniel 4:35)
- sustains all things by His power (Hebrews 1:3)
- works all things according to His purpose (Ephesians 1:11)

This sovereignty does not render God distant or arbitrary. He is neither mechanical nor cruel. His rule is purposeful, wise, and good—even when His ways transcend human understanding.

Reflection and Discussion

1. How does God's sovereignty challenge common ideas about human control and independence?
2. Why must God be sovereign for salvation to be secure?
3. How does God's sovereignty bring comfort rather than fear?

Section 3 - God Is Holy in His Being

God's holiness is one of the most neglected—and most essential—truths in understanding salvation. To say God is holy means that He is morally pure, utterly sinless, and completely set apart from all that He has made.[3]

God's holiness means that He is morally pure, utterly free from sin, and infinitely set apart from all that He has created. God is not simply a greater version of humanity. He is wholly other. Holiness is a defining attribute of God's nature.

> "Holy, holy, holy is the LORD of hosts; the whole earth is full of His glory!"
> —Isaiah 6:3

God's holiness is not simply what He possesses; it is who He is. When the prophet Isaiah encountered the holiness of God, his response was not confidence but collapse.

> "Woe is me! For I am lost; for I am a man of unclean lips."
> —Isaiah 6:5

God's holiness exposes human sinfulness. It reveals that sin is not minor, accidental, or excusable—but offensive to a holy God.

Without understanding God's holiness:

- Sin seems small
- Judgment seems excessive
- Grace seems unnecessary

But when God's holiness is rightly seen, salvation becomes precious.

Reflection and Discussion

1. Why do you think God's holiness is often downplayed today?
2. How does God's holiness change the way you view sin?
3. Why must holiness come before grace in understanding salvation?

Section 4 - God Is Righteous and Just

Because God is holy, He is also righteous and just. His law flows from His character, and His judgments are the expression of His moral perfection.[4]

> "The LORD is righteous in all His ways."
> —Psalm 145:17

God never acts unjustly. He does not ignore sin, excuse guilt, or compromise righteousness. Sin is not merely unfortunate behavior or human weakness—it is rebellion against the righteous authority of God.

If God were to ignore sin, excuse guilt, or suspend justice, He would deny His own nature. This creates a serious problem for humanity. If God is just, sin must be judged. Salvation cannot mean that God simply relaxes His standards. Any true salvation must satisfy God's justice, not bypass it.

This truth prepares us for the necessity of the cross—where justice and mercy meet.

Reflection &Discussion

1. Why is justice an essential part of God's goodness?
2. How does God's justice make salvation necessary rather than optional?
3. Why can grace never come at the expense of righteousness?

Section 5 - God Is Triune: Father, Son, and Holy Spirit

Because salvation is God's work, we must also understand who God is in His inner life. Scripture reveals that the one true God eternally exists as Father, Son, and Holy Spirit—one God in three persons, equal in essence and glory, distinct in personhood, united in purpose.[5]

The Trinity is not an abstract doctrine—
it is the heartbeat of salvation.

This truth appears throughout Scripture. The Father lovingly sends the Son into the world (John 3:16). The Son reveals the Father (John 1:18) and accomplishes redemption through His obedient life, atoning death, and victorious resurrection. The Holy Spirit then applies the finished work of Christ to the hearts of sinners—opening blind eyes, giving spiritual life, and drawing people to faith (John 16:7–15; Romans 8:11).

- The Father plans redemption.
- The Son accomplishes redemption.
- The Spirit applies redemption.

The baptism of Jesus offers one of the clearest pictures of this triune work. As the Son stands in the water, the Spirit descends upon Him like a dove, and the Father declares from heaven, "This is My beloved Son" (Matthew 3:16–17). All three persons of God act in perfect unity, revealing one divine nature and one saving purpose.

- The Father speaks from heaven.
- The Son stands in the water.
- The Spirit descends like a dove.

The doctrine of the Trinity is not an abstract theological concept—it is the heartbeat of salvation. Only the Father could lovingly plan redemption. Only the Son could accomplish redemption. Only the Spirit could apply redemption. Without the Trinity, there is no gospel. With the Trinity, salvation is the overflow of God's eternal love shared among Father, Son, and Spirit, now extended to sinners through grace.

Salvation is not the work of one person of the Trinity acting alone, but the unified work of the Triune God. Without the Trinity, there is no gospel.

Reflection & Discussion

1. Why is the Trinity essential to understanding salvation?
2. How does each person of the Trinity contribute to redemption?
3. How does this deepen your understanding of God's love and grace?

Chapter Summary

Salvation begins with God:

- A sovereign God who reigns
- A holy God who cannot tolerate sin
- A righteous God who must judge guilt
- A Triune God who saves sinners through grace

Why This Matters for Salvation

The holiness, righteousness, and sovereignty of God establish the framework for everything that follows. Salvation does not begin with human worth, potential, or effort, but with the character of God Himself. Until God is rightly understood, salvation cannot be rightly explained.

A holy God cannot ignore sin.
A righteous God must judge guilt.
A sovereign God must save in a way that glorifies His name.

These truths prepare us for the sobering reality addressed next: if God is as holy and righteous as Scripture declares, then the condition of humanity before Him must be taken seriously.

In the next chapter, we will examine:
Sin, judgment, and the true condition of the human heart—and why salvation is absolutely necessary.

Chapter 1 Endnotes

1. Scripture begins with God's self-revelation and supremacy, grounding all theology in who He is and what He has done (Genesis 1:1; Psalm 99:1–3; Romans 11:36).
2. God's sovereignty is comprehensive and purposeful, governing history, nations, and every event according to His will, without being threatened or overturned (Daniel 4:35; Ephesians 1:11; Psalm 115:3; Hebrews 1:3).
3. God's holiness includes moral purity and absolute otherness—He is sinless, set apart, and incomparable as Creator, which exposes human uncleanness in His presence (Isaiah 6:3–5; Isaiah 40:25; Revelation 4:8).
4. God's righteousness and justice require that sin be judged, and the gospel uniquely displays the harmony of justice and mercy through Christ's atoning work (Romans 6:23; Romans 3:25–26; Psalm 145:17).
5. God is one God in three persons—Father, Son, and Holy Spirit—working in unity in redemption, with clear triune patterns in Scripture (Matthew 3:16–17; Matthew 28:19; John 16:7–15; 2 Corinthians 13:14; Romans 8:11).

CHAPTER 2

SIN, JUDGMENT, AND THE HUMAN CONDITION

Why Salvation Is Necessary

Chapter Overview

To understand the seriousness of sin, the reality of judgment, and humanity's complete inability to save itself.

If God is holy, righteous, and sovereign, then the condition of humanity before Him must be taken with utmost seriousness. Scripture diagnoses the human problem not as a lack of education, opportunity, or moral refinement, but as **sin**—a deep, pervasive corruption of the human heart that renders all people guilty and unable to save themselves.

> "For all have sinned and fall short of the glory of God."
> —Romans 3:23

Sin is universal. No one escapes its reach. Every human being stands accountable before God and in desperate need of salvation.

Why This Chapter Matters

Until sin is seen rightly:

- Grace is minimized
- The cross is misunderstood
- Salvation becomes unnecessary

Section 1 - The Origin of Sin

The Bible presents sin as entering the world through a real, historical act of disobedience. God created Adam and Eve upright, placed them in a good creation, and gave them a clear and gracious command.[1]

> "You may surely eat of every tree of the garden, but of the tree of the knowledge of good and evil you shall not eat."
> —Genesis 2:16–17

This command was not arbitrary. It established God as Creator and Lord, and humanity as dependent and accountable. When Adam disobeyed, sin entered the world—bringing with it guilt, corruption, and death.

> "Therefore, just as sin came into the world through one man, and death through sin, so death spread to all men because all sinned."
> —Romans 5:12

Adam's fall was not merely personal. As the covenant head of humanity, his disobedience brought condemnation upon all who have descended from him. Humanity's problem is therefore not merely that people commit individual sins, but that they are born into a fallen condition under Adam's representative guilt and corruption.

Reflection & Discussion

1. Why does Scripture emphasize Adam's role?

2. How does this challenge the idea that people are born morally neutral?
3. Why does this make salvation a necessity rather than a preference?

Section 2 - The Nature of Sin

Sin is far more than isolated wrong actions or moral missteps. Scripture presents sin as a deep and pervasive condition that shapes the entire human person. At its core, sin is lawlessness—living in defiance of God's rightful authority (1 John 3:4). It is rebellion against the Creator, a rejection of His rule and His ways (Isaiah 1:2). Sin is not merely something we do; it is something we are by nature.[2]

Sin is more than wrong actions—it is a condition of the heart.

> "The heart is deceitful above all things, and desperately sick; who can understand it?"
> —Jeremiah 17:9

This diagnosis reveals that sin is internal before it is external. Human hearts are not morally neutral or spiritually intact—they are corrupt, self-deceptive, and inclined away from God. Because sin flows from the heart, outward behavior is only the visible expression of a deeper inward problem.

Sin affects:

- The mind
- The will

- The affections
- The conscience

As a result, sin affects every aspect of human nature. The mind is darkened and unable to rightly perceive spiritual truth. The will is bent away from God and resistant to His authority. The affections are disordered, loving what God hates and neglecting what He loves. Even the conscience becomes corrupted and unreliable. Scripture therefore speaks of sin not only as guilt, but as spiritual death—a condition of separation from the life of God (Isaiah 59:2, Ephesians 2:1).

This comprehensive corruption is often described as total—not in the sense that people are as evil as they could possibly be, but in the sense that sin reaches every part of who we are. No faculty of human nature remains untouched. Humanity is not merely weakened by sin but fundamentally distorted by it.[3]

Reflection & Discussion

1. Why is it important to see sin as a condition, not just actions?
2. How does this challenge self-improvement approaches to salvation?
3. Why must salvation involve new life, not just forgiveness?

Section 3 - The Universality of Sin

Scripture leaves no room for exceptions when diagnosing the human condition. Sin is not limited to certain groups, cultures, or degrees of morality; it applies universally.

"None is righteous, no, not one." - Romans 3:10

Regardless of background, education, culture, or moral upbringing, every person shares the same spiritual condition apart from Christ. Sin is not confined to those who outwardly reject religion or openly pursue immorality. Religious people sin. Moral people sin. Irreligious people sin. Even sincere people sin. Sincerity, discipline, and moral restraint cannot remove guilt before a holy God.

This is because sin is not measured solely by outward behavior, but by the inward disposition of the heart. God's standard is not external conformity, but perfect righteousness from the inside out. His judgment penetrates beneath actions into motives, desires, and thoughts. When measured against God's holiness, all fall short—not merely in conduct, but in nature. No one stands righteous before God by nature.

The universality of sin eliminates every ground for human boasting. No one possesses a moral advantage before God. All stand equally guilty, equally helpless, and equally dependent upon grace.

Reflection & Discussion

1. Why does Scripture remove all grounds for boasting?
2. How does this unify humanity under the need for grace?
3. Why does sincerity not remove guilt?

Section 4 - The Consequences of Sin

Sin always brings death. Scripture describes death not merely as the end of physical life, but as a multifaceted judgment that touches every dimension of human existence.

> "For the wages of sin is death." —Romans 6:23

Sin brings:

- Spiritual death
- Physical death
- Eternal judgment

First, humanity is born in a state of spiritual death—separated from the life of God.

> "And you were dead in the trespasses and sins…"
> —Ephesians 2:1

Spiritual death is not simply moral weakness or poor decision-making; it is an inability.[4]

Those who are spiritually dead cannot seek God, please Him, or submit to His will. Left to themselves, sinners lack both the desire and the capacity to respond rightly to God. Without divine intervention, spiritual life is impossible.

Second, sin introduced physical death into God's creation.

> "By a man came death."
> —1 Corinthians 15:21

Physical death was not part of God's original design but entered the world through the sin of one man, Adam. Death is an intruder—a persistent reminder that creation itself has been subjected to corruption.

Finally, apart from redemption, sin results in eternal death—everlasting separation from God under His righteous judgment.

> "These will go away into eternal punishment, but the righteous into eternal life."
> —Matthew 25:46

Taken together, the consequences of sin reveal the full gravity of humanity's condition. Sin brings death now, death in the body, and death forever. The problem is total, not temporary. Only a salvation that overcomes spiritual death, conquers physical death, and rescues from eternal judgment can truly save.

Reflection & Discussion

1. Why does Scripture describe sinners as "dead," not merely sick?
2. How does this shape our understanding of salvation?
3. Why must salvation address death, not just behavior?
4. Which consequence of sin is most often minimized today?
5. Why must salvation come from God, not from within us?

Section 5 - God's Righteous Judgment

Because God is holy and just, He must judge sin. Judgment is not an unfortunate side effect of God's character, but a necessary expression of His righteousness. Judgment is not cruelty—it is righteousness expressed.[5]

> "It is appointed for man to die once, and after that comes judgment."
> —Hebrews 9:27

Human life moves inevitably toward a divine reckoning. God's judgment is never arbitrary. Nothing is hidden, altered, or overlooked. Unlike human courts, His judgments are perfectly informed, impartial, and just. His judgments are unavoidable.

> "All things are naked and exposed to the eyes of Him to whom we must give account."
> —Hebrews 4:13

Every thought, motive, word, and deed stands fully revealed before Him.

God's judgment is:

- Righteous
- Impartial
- Inescapable
- Final

Scripture repeatedly emphasizes several defining truths about divine judgment. God's judgment is **righteous** because it flows from His holy nature. It is **impartial**, measured not by status, power, or moral appearance but by truth. It is **inescapable**, for no human being can flee from God's presence or authority. And it is **final**, leaving no room for appeal apart from the mercy God Himself provides.

God's judgment, however, must be understood rightly. It is not the cruelty of a tyrant, but the justice of the holy King. If God were to ignore sin or compromise His justice, He would deny His own nature. Judgment is not contrary to God's goodness; it is an essential expression of it.

Reflection & Discussion

1. Why is judgment necessary for justice?
2. How does this magnify the mercy of the Gospel?
3. Why is grace meaningful only in light of judgment?

Section 6 - Humanity's Inability to Save Itself

If sin has corrupted the human heart and placed all people under God's judgment, the question naturally arises: can humanity fix this condition on its own? Scripture answers unequivocally—no. The problem of sin lies too deep.

> "Those who are in the flesh cannot please God."
> —Romans 8:8

Scripture consistently denies that salvation can be achieved through moral reform, religious effort, intellectual agreement, or sincere intentions. No amount of good work can erase guilt.

No religious observance can compensate for rebellion. No sincerity can substitute for righteousness. Even the most outwardly moral life falls short when measured against the perfect standard of God's law.

This is not a statement about effort, but about ability. Apart from God's gracious intervention, sinners are incapable of submitting to God, desiring His glory, or returning to Him rightly. The natural person may appear ethical or religious yet remain spiritually dead and alienated from God.

This inability does not imply maximal wickedness or incapable of outward goodness. Rather, it speaks to the nature of man. Apart from grace, no one seeks God as He must be sought.

> "No one seeks for God."
> —Romans 3:11

Salvation, therefore, cannot originate from within humanity. It cannot be earned, achieved, or coerced into existence. It must come from outside—from God Himself.

Reflection & Discussion

1. Why does inability differ from unwillingness?
2. How does this preserve grace?
3. Why must salvation come from outside humanity?

Section 7 - The Necessity of Grace (Why Salvation Must Come From God Alone)

Humanity's inability to save itself does not lead to despair—it establishes necessity. If sinners are truly guilty before a holy God, spiritually dead in sin, and powerless to return to Him on their own, then salvation must come entirely from outside themselves. Any hope of rescue must originate not in human effort, moral reform, or religious activity, but in divine mercy.

Scripture does not present grace as God's help to those who are already capable. It presents grace as God's rescue of the helpless.

> "But God, being rich in mercy, because of the great love with which He loved us, even when we were dead in our trespasses, made us alive together with Christ."
> —Ephesians 2:4–5

Grace is not assistance—it is **rescue**.
Grace is not cooperation—it is **resurrection**.

Until sinners understand the depth of their sin and inability, grace will always seem unnecessary or exaggerated. But once the seriousness of sin is rightly grasped, grace is no longer viewed as an optional spiritual aid—it is recognized as the only possible hope.

The Bible teaches that salvation begins not with human initiative, but with God's merciful intervention. God does not wait for sinners to take the first step toward Him; He acts decisively to bring the spiritually dead to life. This truth strips away pride, silences self-reliance, and prepares the heart to receive salvation as a gift rather than an achievement.

Understanding the necessity of grace also protects the gospel from distortion. If salvation required even partial human contribution, grace would no longer be grace. Scripture insists that salvation is God's work from beginning to end—planned by the Father, accomplished by the Son, and applied by the Holy Spirit.

Only when sinners abandon hope in themselves are they ready to trust fully in the Savior God has provided.

This prepares us for the central question of the gospel:
If salvation must come entirely by grace, how has God accomplished it?

To answer that, we must turn to the person and work of Jesus Christ.

Reflection & Discussion

1. Why does a proper understanding of sin make grace necessary rather than optional?
2. How does Scripture's description of spiritual death challenge the idea that humans can initiate their own salvation?
3. Why must salvation be entirely God's initiative in order to truly be grace?
4. How does this section prepare us to understand why Christ's work is essential and sufficient?

Chapter Summary

Humanity stands guilty before a holy God—sinful by nature, accountable for rebellion, unable to save itself, and facing righteous judgment. Salvation is not optional or supplemental; it is absolutely necessary. Only divine grace can remedy the human condition.

If humanity cannot save itself, the question becomes unavoidable:

Who can save sinners, and how?

The answer to that question centers on one person alone—the Lord Jesus Christ.

Chapter 2 Endnotes

1. Adam's role as representative head of humanity explains how sin and death spread to all people (Romans 5:12–19).
2. Scripture presents sin as both guilt and corruption, affecting the whole person (Genesis 6:5; Ephesians 4:18).
3. Total corruption does not imply maximal wickedness, but comprehensive moral inability apart from grace (Romans 3:9–18).
4. Spiritual death describes separation from God and inability to respond positively to Him (Ephesians 2:1–3).
5. Scripture consistently affirms God's judgment as just, impartial, and unavoidable (Hebrews 9:27; Romans 2:5–6).

CHAPTER 3

THE PERSON OF CHRIST
TRUE GOD AND TRUE MAN

Chapter Overview

To understand who Jesus Christ is, why His identity is essential to salvation, and why Christianity stands or falls on the truth that Jesus is fully God and fully man.

If humanity stands guilty before a holy God and is incapable of self-rescue, then salvation depends entirely on the one God Himself provides. Christianity, therefore, rises or falls on the person of Jesus Christ. If Jesus is not who Scripture proclaims Him to be, then salvation collapses. The gospel is not first a message about what God does, but about who Christ is. Before we consider His work, we must understand His person.

> "For in Him the whole fullness of deity dwells bodily."
> —Colossians 2:9

Why The Person of Christ Matters

Christianity is not built first on a moral code, a religious system, or a spiritual experience—it is built on a **person**. Before asking ***what Christ did***, Scripture demands that we understand ***who Christ is***.

If Jesus were merely a teacher, He could instruct but not save. If He were only a prophet, He could warn but not redeem.

If He were less than God, He would lack authority and infinite worth.

If He were less than man, He could not represent us.

Jesus Christ is not a mere teacher, prophet, or moral example. He is the eternal Son of God who took on human flesh. Scripture presents Him as one person with two natures—fully God and fully man—united without confusion, change, division, or separation.

Reflection & Discussion

1. Why do you think people are often comfortable talking about what Jesus taught but uncomfortable discussing who He claimed to be?
2. How does misunderstanding Christ's identity affect assurance of salvation?

Section 1 – The Eternal Son of God

Jesus Christ did not begin at His birth. Scripture teaches that He existed eternally with the Father before the world was made.[1]

> "In the beginning was the Word, and the Word was with God, and the Word was God."
> —John 1:1

Jesus is not a created being. He is the eternal Word through whom all things were made.

> "All things were made through Him, and without Him was not anything made that was made."
> —John 1:3

As the eternal Son, Jesus shares the same divine nature as the Father and the Spirit. He is coequal, coeternal, and consubstantial with God. Before He entered history, before He assumed flesh, He already existed in glory as the Son of God.

Reflection & Discussion

1. Why is it essential that Jesus did not "come into existence" at Bethlehem?
2. How does Christ's eternality affect His authority over your life?

Section 2 - The Full Deity of Christ

Scripture unmistakably teaches that Jesus Christ possesses the full nature and authority of God Himself.[2]

The New Testament does not present Him merely as God-like or divinely empowered, but as truly and fully God. Titles, actions, attributes, and worship that belong to God alone are repeatedly and unambiguously attributed to Jesus.

Jesus is explicitly called God in Scripture. When the risen Christ appeared to Thomas, he responded in worship, declaring,

> "My Lord and my God!"
> —John 20:28

Elsewhere, Jesus is described as

> "our great God and Savior"
> —Titus 2:13

Such language would be blasphemous if applied to a mere creature. Yet Scripture applies it directly to Christ without hesitation.

Jesus also receives worship—something Scripture strictly reserves for God alone. When the disciples worshiped Him after He calmed the storm (Matthew 14:33), Jesus did not rebuke them, as angels and prophets consistently do elsewhere in scripture. He accepted their worship, affirming His divine identity.

Christ exercises divine authority as well. He forgives sins by His own authority (Mark 2:5–12), rightly provoking outrage from the scribes, who understood that only God can forgive sins. Jesus responded not by denying their premise, but by proving His authority—demonstrating that He is God in the flesh. After His resurrection, He declared,

> "All authority in heaven and on earth has been given to Me."
> —Matthew 28:18

—an all-encompassing claim no created being could make.

Scripture further attributes to Jesus divine attributes that belong to God alone. He is immutable and eternal.

> "Jesus Christ is the same yesterday and today and forever."
> —Hebrews 13:8

Such immutability belongs solely to God, who alone is eternally steady and unaltered by time or circumstance.

To deny the deity of Christ is therefore to deny the gospel itself. Only God can save sinners. Only God can bear the infinite weight of divine justice. Only God can reconcile humanity to Himself. If Jesus were not fully God, His sacrifice would lack infinite worth. But because Christ is truly God, His saving work is sufficient, final, and eternally effective.

Reflection and Discussion

1. Why would Christ's death be insufficient if He were not fully God?
2. How does recognizing Jesus as God confront modern ideas of a "safe" or "tolerable" Jesus?

Section 3 – The Incarnation: God Became Man

At the heart of the Christian gospel stands the truth of the incarnation—that the eternal Son of God took on human flesh.[3]

> "And the Word became flesh and dwelt among us."
> —John 1:14

Salvation does not rest merely on God acting *for* humanity, but on God entering fully *into* humanity in the person of Jesus Christ. The incarnation does not mean that Christ ceased to be God. Nor does it suggest that He merely appeared human. Rather, the eternal Word truly became man while remaining fully God. Jesus never stopped being God. He **took on human nature** while remaining fully divine.

This occurred according to God's appointed time and purpose.

> "When the fullness of time had come, God sent forth His Son, born of woman, born under the law."
> —Galatians 4:4

By being born under the law, Christ placed Himself within the very framework that condemns sinners—not as a transgressor, but as a perfect law-keeper. Salvation required a Savior who could truly represent humanity and possess the divine power necessary to save. Only one who is both God and man could reconcile God and humanity. This was necessary because salvation required:

- A **human representative** who could obey the law
- A **divine Savior** with infinite worth

In the incarnation, God did not rescue humanity from a distance. He came near. He entered history, took on flesh, shared human weakness, and walked among the people He came to redeem.

Reflection & Discussion

1. Why was it necessary for Christ to be born "under the law"?
2. How does the incarnation shape your understanding of God's love?

Section 4 - The Real Humanity of Christ

The incarnation means that Jesus Christ truly and fully became human. He was born, grew, learned, and lived as a real human being, sharing in all the ordinary realities of human life—yet without sin.

Jesus grew in wisdom and stature (Luke 2:52), experienced hunger (Matthew 4:2), fatigue (John 4:6), sorrow and anguish (Matthew 26:38), and grief (John 11:35). These are not the experiences of an illusion, but of genuine humanity.

Scripture also affirms that Christ was tempted as we are.

> "We do not have a high priest who is unable to sympathize with our weaknesses, but one who in every respect has been tempted as we are, yet without sin."
> —Hebrews 4:15

The humanity of Christ was not incidental to salvation—it was necessary. Humanity required a Savior who could truly represent them—one who could obey where Adam failed, suffer where sinners deserve judgment, and die a real human death. At the same time, salvation required divine power and infinite worth. Only one who is both fully God and fully man could reconcile God and humanity.

> "Therefore He had to be made like His brothers in every respect."
> —Hebrews 2:17

Because Christ is truly human, He represents sinners, sympathizes with weakness, and faithfully intercedes for His people. He did not redeem humanity from afar but entered fully into the depths of human life to redeem it.

Reflection & Discussion

1. Why is Christ's humanity essential for substitution?
2. How does Christ's ability to sympathize affect your prayer life?

Section 5 – The Virgin Birth and the Sinlessness of Christ

Jesus Christ was conceived by the Holy Spirit and born of the Virgin Mary.[4]

> "The Holy Spirit will come upon you… therefore the child to be born will be called holy."
> —Luke 1:35

This was not a theological ornament, but a redemptive necessity. Through Adam, guilt and corruption entered the human race. For Christ to be a true Savior, He had to share fully in our humanity—yet without inheriting Adam's guilt or corruption. Christ could not be conceived through a fallen human father and remain sinless. He would have stood under the same condemnation as the rest of humanity and would have needed redemption Himself.

The virgin birth safeguards Christ's true humanity while preserving Him from inherited sin. By being born of a woman, Jesus truly entered the human family. By being conceived by the Holy Spirit, He was preserved from inherited sin.

As a result, Scripture testifies uniformly to Christ's sinlessness.

> "He committed no sin, neither was deceit found in His mouth."
> —1 Peter 2:22

Only a spotless Savior could offer a perfect sacrifice. Only a sinless substitute could bear the sins of others. The virgin birth protects the gospel by preserving Christ's deity, humanity, and sinlessness.

Reflection & Discussion

1. Why could a sinful Savior not save sinners?
2. How does Christ's sinlessness provide confidence in salvation?

Section 6 - One Person, Two Natures

Jesus Christ is one person with two distinct natures—divine and human—united forever without confusion, change, division, or separation.[5]

This means Jesus is not partly God and partly man, nor two persons acting side by side. He is fully God and fully man in one person—the eternal Son who assumed human nature without surrendering His divine nature.

Because of this union, everything Jesus does is the act of **one person**.

The same Jesus who hungered, wept, and suffered is the eternal Son through whom all things were created. The one who slept from exhaustion in a boat is the Lord God who commands the wind and waves. Because His two natures are united in one person, Christ's actions possess both genuine human reality and divine power.

This truth is essential for salvation.

- **As man**, Christ represents humanity, obeys God's law in our place, and dies a real human death.
- **As God**, His obedience has infinite worth and His sacrifice fully satisfies divine justice.

Scripture affirms this mystery:

> "Great indeed, we confess, is the mystery of godliness: He was manifested in the flesh."
> —1 Timothy 3:16

Because Christ is one person with two natures, everything He does—His obedience, His suffering, and His death—is the saving act of the one eternal Son. As a man, He obeys the law and dies a real human death. As God, His obedience has infinite worth, and His sacrifice satisfies divine justice. For this reason, He alone is qualified to reconcile God and humanity, standing uniquely between heaven and earth as the one true mediator.

The incarnation remains a mystery—not because it is irrational, but because it surpasses human comprehension. Yet it is precisely this union of divine and human natures that enables Christ to serve as the one and only Savior.

Reflection & Discussion

1. Does the idea of two natures prevent us from seeing Jesus as one unified person?
2. In what ways does Jesus's life, as both God and Man, serve as a model for Christian living?
3. How would you explain the "Hypostatic Union" (one Person, two natures) to someone unfamiliar with it?

Section 7 - Why The Person of Christ Matters

Everything the gospel proclaims depends on who Christ is. If Jesus were not fully God and fully man, salvation as Scripture describes it would be impossible.

If Christ were not fully God, His life and death would lack infinite worth. Only God Himself possesses the authority to forgive sins, the power to conquer death, and the worth necessary to secure eternal redemption.

If Christ were not fully man, He could not truly represent humanity. He could not obey God's law as a human substitute, suffer in the place of sinners, or die a real human death. Redemption required not only divine power, but human obedience and human suffering offered in the place of the guilty.

Because Jesus Christ is both true God and true man, He stands uniquely qualified to reconcile God and humanity.

> "There is one mediator between God and men, the man Christ Jesus."
> —1 Timothy 2:5

As God, He brings God to humanity. As man, He brings humanity to God. In His one person, heaven and earth meet. He alone stands between heaven and earth.

Christ's person is the foundation of assurance. His eternal deity secures the permanence of salvation. His real humanity ensures His sympathy and representation. His sinlessness guarantees His righteousness. His unchanging identity guarantees the unchanging effectiveness of His work.

Christianity does not begin with human effort or spiritual experience. It begins with a person—the Lord Jesus Christ. Because He is who Scripture proclaims Him to be, salvation is not uncertain but finished; not fragile but secure.

If Christ were not fully God, His work would lack infinite worth. If Christ were not fully man, He could not represent sinners. Because He is both, salvation is complete, sufficient, and secure.

Christianity does not begin with human effort—it begins with Christ.

Reflection & Discussion

1. Why is Christ uniquely qualified to be the mediator?
2. How does this truth protect assurance?
3. What does it mean that Jesus is the "God-Man," and how does that differ from being a blended being?
4. Did Jesus give up His divine attributes when He became man, or did He simply choose not to use them?
5. Who do you say Jesus is?
6. Is your confidence rooted in Christ's person or your performance?

Chapter Summary

Jesus Christ is the eternal Son of God who became fully man to save sinners. Everything about salvation depends on who He is. Because Christ is truly God and truly man, His work is sufficient, final, and eternally secure.

Preparing For The Next Chapter

Here, I present Christ's mediatorial **identity**. Later, I will elaborate on His salvific **role.** If Christ is truly God and truly man, then the next question naturally follows:

What did this Savior come to accomplish?

In the next chapter, we turn from His person to His work—the heart of redemption.

Chapter 3 Endnotes

1. Scripture teaches the eternal preexistence of Christ as the divine Word (John 1:1–3; Colossians 1:16–17).
2. The deity of Christ is affirmed through divine titles, attributes, and worship given to Him (John 20:28; Hebrews 1:6).
3. The incarnation affirms that Christ took on full humanity without ceasing to be God (John 1:14; Galatians 4:4).
4. The virgin birth safeguards Christ's humanity, deity, and sinlessness (Luke 1:35; Matthew 1:23).
5. Christ's two natures are united in one person, enabling Him to serve as the sole mediator between God and humanity (1 Timothy 2:5).

CHAPTER 4

THE WORK OF CHRIST
REDEMPTION ACCOMPLISHED

Chapter Overview

This chapter explores **what Jesus Christ came to accomplish**. Christianity rests not only on *who Christ is*, but on *what He has done*. The Bible presents Christ's saving work as **complete, sufficient, and final**. Salvation is not made possible by the cross — it is **secured** by it.

By the end of this chapter, participants should understand:

- Why Christ's work is as essential as His person
- What Jesus accomplished through His life, death, resurrection, and exaltation
- Why salvation is **secured**, not merely made possible
- Why Christ alone can save

Why Christ's Work Matters

Many people believe Jesus came primarily to teach moral lessons, inspire compassion, or provide an example to follow. Scripture presents something far more profound.

Jesus did not come merely to **show the way** — He came to **accomplish redemption**.

If Christ's work is misunderstood, salvation becomes uncertain. But if Christ's work is rightly understood, assurance becomes possible.

Christianity rests not only on the identity of Christ, but on His saving work on behalf of sinners. The gospel is not merely that God became man, but that the God-man acted decisively in history to redeem a people for Himself.

Scripture presents Christ's work as purposeful, necessary, sufficient, and final. Jesus did not come simply to teach moral truth, model obedience, or inspire religious devotion. He came to fulfill the law, undo the curse of sin, satisfy divine justice, and reconcile sinners to a holy God. Everything He did—from His obedience in life to His suffering in death—was undertaken with redemption in view.

> "For the Son of Man came to seek and to save the lost."
> —Luke 19:10

The saving work of Christ is not a collection of separate acts, but a unified redemptive mission. His incarnation made redemption possible; His obedience made righteousness available; His death dealt decisively with guilt and judgment; His resurrection secured victory over sin and death; and His exaltation confirms the finality and effectiveness of His work. Each aspect is distinct, yet inseparable from the others.

At the heart of Christ's saving work stands the cross. There, Jesus bore the penalty for sin, absorbed the wrath of God in the place of His people, and accomplished what sinners could never do for themselves. The cross does not make salvation possible—**it secures it**. Christ's work did not create an opportunity for redemption; it achieved redemption.

> "When He had offered for all time a single sacrifice for sins, He sat down at the right hand of God."
> —Hebrews 10:12

To understand why Christ alone can save, we must see how Scripture presents Him as the center of God's eternal redemptive plan. In Scripture, sitting down signifies completion. Christ's work does not continue through repeated sacrifices or human contribution. Nothing remains to be added.

> "There is salvation in no one else, for there is no other name under heaven given among men by which we must be saved."
> —Acts 4:12

Reflection & Discussion

1. Why do you think many people focus on Jesus' teachings but avoid His cross?
2. What happens to the gospel if Christ's work is reduced to example or inspiration?
3. Why do people often assume salvation requires something in addition to Christ's work?
4. How does viewing salvation as "accomplished" affect assurance?

Section 1 - Christ Is the Fulfillment of God's Redemptive Plan

From Genesis to Revelation, Scripture bears witness to one unified redemptive purpose centered on Jesus Christ. Redemption does not unfold as a series of disconnected religious ideas, but as a coherent story authored by God and fulfilled in His Son. Every covenant, promise, sacrifice, and prophecy anticipates the coming of Christ and finds its ultimate meaning in Him.

> "For all the promises of God find their Yes in Him."
> —2 Corinthians 1:20

Christ is not an afterthought, nor God's response to human failure. He is the promised Seed who would crush the serpent, the sacrificial Lamb foreshadowed in Israel's offerings, the faithful Servant who would bear the sins of many, the righteous King who would reign forever, and the conquering Redeemer foretold throughout the Old Testament.

Jesus Himself taught that the entire Scripture pointed to His saving mission.

> "Beginning with Moses and all the Prophets, He interpreted to them in all the Scriptures the things concerning Himself."
> —Luke 24:27

The gospel is therefore not a departure from the Old Testament but its fulfillment. The entire storyline of Scripture converges on Christ alone. The gospel is not a new idea—it is the fulfillment of God's eternal plan.[1]

Reflection & Discussion

1. Why is it important that Christ fulfills God's plan rather than creating a new one?
2. How does this strengthen confidence in the gospel's reliability?

Section 2 - Christ Alone Reveals the Father

Because Christ is the fulfillment of God's redemptive plan, He is also God's definitive revelation. Saving faith is not vague spirituality—it is coming to the Father through the Son. Apart from Christ, sinful humanity does not truly know God.

> "No one has ever seen God; the only God, who is at the Father's side, He has made Him known."
> —John 1:18

Jesus does not merely speak about God—He reveals God fully and perfectly. To see Christ is to see the Father (John 14:9). His words, works, compassion, authority, holiness, and mercy express the character.

This reality has decisive implications: salvation cannot be found in vague spirituality or general belief in a higher power. Saving knowledge of God comes only through the Son.[2]

Why This Matters for Salvation

Salvation is not found in vague spirituality or belief in a higher power. Saving knowledge of God comes **only through the Son**.[2]

To reject Christ is to remain ignorant of God's saving nature.

Reflection & Discussion

1. Why do you think "belief in God" can feel sufficient to many people, even if Christ is absent?
2. Why is knowing about God different from knowing God *through Christ*?
3. How does this challenge common ideas about spirituality?
4. What are practical examples of "vague spirituality" that sound Christian but avoid Christ?
5. When you think of God, what attributes rise first—power, kindness, judgment, distance, mercy?
6. How has Christ corrected or clarified your view of God?

If Christ reveals the Father, then sin is exposed for what it truly is—not a minor flaw, but a holy problem. That leads to the next question:

How can sinners who do not know God rightly be brought near to God truly?

Scripture's answer is not self-improvement but **reconciliation through Christ alone.**

Section 3 - Christ Alone Reconciles Sinners to God

Sin creates more than guilt—it creates separation. Humanity's deepest problem is not ignorance or moral imperfection. but alienation from a holy God. Scripture presents reconciliation not as a human achievement, but as a divine act accomplished solely through Jesus Christ.[3]

> "For in Christ God was reconciling the world to Himself, not counting their trespasses against them."
> —2 Corinthians 5:19

Reconciliation requires that sin be dealt with justly. It cannot be achieved through remorse, moral effort, or religious observance. At the cross, God does not ignore sin—He satisfies His own justice through a substitute. Christ bears the penalty sinners deserve so that peace with God may be established without compromising divine holiness.

The cross, therefore, is not merely a demonstration of love; it is the decisive act by which sinners are lawfully brought near to God.

At the cross:

- God remains just
- Sin is judged
- Peace is established

Because reconciliation is accomplished by Christ, it is *received,* not earned. Those united to Him by faith are no longer enemies but are brought into peace with God—hostility is replaced with fellowship, alienation with adoption, and judgment with grace. Outside of Christ, reconciliation remains impossible. In Him, and Him alone, it is certain and complete.

Reflection & Discussion

1. Why can reconciliation never be achieved through moral effort or sincerity?
2. How does substitution protect both God's justice and God's mercy?

Section 4 - Christ Is the Only Mediator

Scripture allows no rivals in the work of salvation. God has appointed one—and only one—mediator between Himself and sinners:

> "For there is one God, and there is one mediator between God and men, the man Christ Jesus."
> —1 Timothy 2:5

A mediator must fully represent both parties. Only Jesus Christ—true God and true man—possesses the qualifications necessary to bring a holy God and sinful humanity together. Because He is God, He reveals the Father perfectly, bears divine authority, and accomplishes redemption with infinite worth. Because He is man, He stands in humanity's place, obeys the law on their behalf, and bears the penalty their sins deserve.

Christ's mediatorial role is therefore not symbolic or ceremonial. It is real and effectual. He does not merely **point** humanity toward God—He **brings** them to God through His own person and work. He accomplishes reconciliation not by negotiation, but by substitution. At the cross, the Mediator Himself becomes the sacrifice that secures peace between God and sinners.

This truth excludes every alternative path. No priest, saint, sacrament, ritual, or spiritual effort can mediate salvation. The gospel does not operate through layers of intermediaries; it flows directly from God to sinners through His appointed Mediator. Any system that introduces additional mediators diminishes the sufficiency of Christ and contradicts the Scriptures.

Christ's role as mediator is not simply functional—it is grounded in His unique person. As God, His life and death possess infinite worth. As man, His obedience and suffering are offered on behalf of real human beings. In His one person, heaven and earth meet, divine justice is satisfied, and humanity is brought near to God.[4]

Christ's mediatorship prepares us for His own testimony concerning Himself and the exclusive nature of salvation in His name.

Reflection & Discussion

1. Why can no other mediator share Christ's role?
2. How does this protect the sufficiency of the gospel?

Section 5 - Christ's Own Testimony Concerning Himself

Jesus spoke plainly and authoritatively about His identity and mission. He did not present himself as one option among many. He claimed absolute exclusivity.[5]

> "I am the way, and the truth, and the life. No one comes to the Father except through Me."
> —John 14:6

These words are not the claims of a religious guide pointing beyond himself. Jesus does not say He shows the way—**He is the way**. He does not merely teach truth—**He is the truth**. He does not simply offer life—**He is the life**. Access to God is not found through principles, moral effort, spiritual practices, or alternative mediators, but through **personal union with Christ Himself**.

To reject Christ is not merely to decline one religious option—it is to reject the only Savior God has provided. Conversely, to believe in Christ is to receive life, forgiveness, and reconciliation with God. Jesus' own testimony demands a clear conclusion: salvation is centered entirely in Him, and apart from Him there is no access to the Father.

Because Christ is the only mediator, His words carry divine authority—and His exclusive claims about salvation follow naturally from who He is and what He alone can accomplish.

Reflection & Discussion

1. Why do Christ's own words remove the possibility of religious neutrality?
2. How do His claims demand a personal response?

Section 6 - Why the Exclusivity of Christ Matters

If Christ alone can mediate salvation, then salvation must be found in Him alone. Christ's exclusivity is not arrogance—it is necessity. If sinners could save themselves, the incarnation would be unnecessary. If righteousness could be earned, the cross would be excessive. If spiritual sincerity were enough, Christ would not have needed to die.

Jesus' exclusivity flows naturally from His identity. Because He alone reveals the Father perfectly, obeys the law entirely, bears sin fully, and conquers death decisively, He alone can provide salvation.

> "There is salvation in no one else."
> —Acts 4:12

To approach God apart from Christ is not another path—it is no path at all. Salvation is not achieved by sincerity, religious devotion, or philosophical reflection, but by coming to God through the Son He has sent.

Throughout His ministry, Jesus reinforced this truth. He declared that eternal life belongs to those who believe in Him (John 3:16), that forgiveness flows through His authority alone

(Mark 2:10), and that final judgment depends upon one's response to Him (John 5:22–24). These claims leave no room for neutrality. To encounter Christ is to be confronted with a decision concerning truth, life, and eternal destiny.

Reflection & Discussion

1. Why does exclusivity magnify grace rather than restrict it?
2. How does this shape the church's message to the world?

Chapter Summary

Jesus Christ fulfilled God's redemptive plan, revealed the Father, reconciled sinners, and secured salvation through His finished work. Redemption is not potential — it is accomplished. Salvation rests not on what we do, but on what Christ has done.

Preparing For The Next Chapter

If Christ has accomplished redemption fully and finally, the next question becomes unavoidable:

How does His finished work become ours?

In the next chapter, we will examine how salvation is **received** — through repentance and faith — and why even our response to the gospel is grounded in God's grace.

Chapter 4 Endnotes

1. Christ fulfills the whole arc of God's redemptive promises (Luke 24:27; 2 Cor. 1:20).
2. Christ uniquely reveals the Father and makes Him known (John 1:18; John 14:9).
3. Reconciliation is accomplished solely through Christ's atoning work (2 Cor. 5:18–21).
4. Christ alone mediates salvation because of His divine–human person (1 Tim. 2:5; Heb. 7:25).
5. Christ's exclusive claims demonstrate the necessity of faith in Him alone (John 14:6; Acts 4:12).

CHAPTER 5

THE GOSPEL CALL AND THE RESPONSE OF FAITH

Redemption Received

Christ's saving work is complete, sufficient, and final. Nothing can be added to what He has accomplished, and nothing remains undone. Yet Scripture makes clear that the gospel is not merely a message to be observed or admired—it is a summons from God that demands a response. The accomplished work of Christ must be personally received by sinners through repentance and faith.[1]

Because Christ stands as the only Savior ordained by God, neutrality is impossible. The gospel confronts every sinner with a decisive reality—not whether salvation exists, but whether they will receive the salvation God has provided in His Son.

> "Whoever believes in the Son has eternal life; whoever does not obey the Son shall not see life."
> —John 3:36

When Scripture calls sinners to "believe" in Jesus Christ, it describes the Spirit-enabled response of a heart awakened by grace. Biblical belief is not mere intellectual agreement with facts about Jesus, nor is it a human decision that initiates salvation. It is the trusting response of a sinner who has been brought from death to life.

To believe in Christ is to receive Him as He is offered in the gospel—fully and freely. It is to rest entirely upon His finished work, abandoning all self-reliance and hope in personal righteousness. Faith does not contribute to salvation; it receives salvation.

This faith necessarily includes repentance. Repentance and faith are distinct but inseparable aspects of the same grace-enabled response. Faith turns toward Christ; repentance turns away from sin. Neither earns salvation, and neither exists without the other. Both flow from God's regenerating work in the heart.[4]

In this sense, belief involves surrender—not as a condition that secures salvation, but as the posture of genuine trust. To trust Christ is to yield oneself to Him, acknowledging His authority and mercy. This surrender is not a promise of future obedience, but the acknowledgment that Christ alone is Lord and Savior.

Scripture therefore contrasts belief not with doubt, but with disobedience: "whoever does not obey the Son shall not see life." (John 3:36)

Unbelief is not merely intellectual uncertainty; it is the refusal to come to Christ in trusting submission. Belief, by contrast, is the grace-enabled response of a heart that has been made willing to receive Him.

In Chapter 7, we will see how repentance and faith fit within God's saving order—not as causes of regeneration, but as the immediate fruits of new life given by the Holy Spirit.

The call of the gospel is both gracious and authoritative. God commands all people everywhere to repent and believe—not because salvation depends on human effort, but because Christ has already accomplished everything necessary for salvation.

This call does not invite sinners to reform themselves, contribute to redemption, or improve their standing before God. It calls them to abandon all self-reliance and entrust themselves wholly to Christ.

Scripture consistently presents repentance and faith not as meritorious works, but as the God-appointed means by which sinners receive Christ and all His saving benefits. To reject Christ is to remain under judgment; to receive Him is to pass from death to life.

> "Repent and believe in the gospel."
> —Mark 1:15

Reflection & Discussion

1. Why is it important to understand that the gospel is not merely information to admire, but a summons that calls for a response?
2. How does this protect us from treating Christianity as theoretical rather than personal?)

3. How does Scripture's use of the word "believe" challenge the idea that faith is only intellectual agreement?
4. What elements of trust, dependence, and reception are present in biblical faith?
5. Why is it essential to hold together both repentance and faith without confusing them or separating them?
6. What happens if repentance is emphasized without faith—or faith without repentance?
7. John 3:36 contrasts belief with disobedience rather than with doubt. How does this shape your understanding of unbelief?
8. Why is unbelief more than uncertainty or lack of information?
9. What does it mean to say that surrender is the posture of genuine faith, not a condition for earning salvation?
10. Having seen what Christ has accomplished for sinners, we now consider how that finished work is received by sinners—through repentance toward God and faith in the Lord Jesus Christ.

Section 1 - The Gospel Call

The gospel call is God's authoritative invitation to sinners to come to Christ for salvation. It is not a suggestion, negotiation, or mere offer of assistance, but a royal summons issued by the King Himself. Scripture proclaims that God commands repentance and faith because salvation is found nowhere else.[1]

> "God commands all people everywhere to repent."
> —Acts 17:30

The gospel call goes forth through the proclamation of God's Word. When the gospel is preached, God Himself is calling sinners to turn from sin and trust in His Son. This call is sincere and universal—addressed to all without distinction—yet it is grounded entirely in what Christ has already accomplished.

The gospel does not ask sinners to prepare themselves for salvation, contribute to their redemption, or make themselves worthy of grace. It declares that salvation has been accomplished and calls sinners to receive it by turning to Christ.

Reflection & Discussion

1. Why is it important to understand the gospel call as authoritative, not optional?
2. How does viewing the gospel as a command challenge common ideas about salvation?
3. In what ways might people misunderstand the gospel as an offer of "help" rather than a call to surrender?
4. When you hear the gospel, do you think primarily in terms of what God has done, or what you must do?

Section 2 - Repentance Toward God

Repentance is an essential component of the biblical response to the gospel. It is not a work that earns salvation, but a necessary turning that accompanies true faith. Scripture presents repentance as a profound change of mind and heart that results in a changed direction of life.[2]

> "God has granted repentance that leads to life."
> —Acts 11:18

Repentance involves recognizing sin for what it truly is—not merely personal failure or moral weakness, but rebellion against God. It includes sorrow for offending a Holy God, confession of guilt, and a decisive turning away from sin toward obedience to God. True repentance does not merely regret consequences; it grieves offense against a holy God.

Importantly, repentance is a gift of grace, not a self-generated human achievement. Scripture teaches that repentance is a gift from God. This safeguards the gospel from legalism. Repentance does not qualify a sinner for grace; it is the fruit of grace already at work in the heart.

> "If perhaps God may grant them repentance leading to a knowledge of the truth."
> —2 Timothy 2:25

Reflection & Discussion

1. How does Scripture distinguish repentance from regret or remorse?
2. Why is it important that repentance is described as a **gift from God**?
3. How does this understanding protect the gospel from legalism?

4. Is there any area of sin you tend to excuse rather than repent of? What might genuine repentance look like there?

Section 3 - Faith in the Lord Jesus Christ

Faith is personal trust in Jesus Christ alone for salvation. It is not mere intellectual agreement with biblical facts, nor is it emotional experience or religious optimism. Saving faith rests entirely in the person and finished work of Christ.[3]

> "By grace you have been saved through faith."
> —Ephesians 2:8

Faith looks away from self and clings to Christ. It receives Him as He is offered in the gospel—Prophet, Priest, and King. True faith trusts Christ's obedience rather than personal morality, Christ's sacrifice rather than human effort, and Christ's righteousness rather than self-righteousness.

Faith does not add to Christ's work; it **receives** it. It does not complete salvation; it **rests** in what has already been completed. Even faith itself is a gift of grace, not a ground for boasting.

> "It has been granted to you that for the sake of Christ you should… believe in Him."
> —Philippians 1:29

Reflection & Discussion

1. How does biblical faith differ from simply "believing in God"?
2. Why is it important that faith rests on **who Christ is and what He has done**, not on its own strength?
3. How does understanding faith as a gift deepen assurance?
4. When doubts arise, do you examine **your faith**, or do you look again to **Christ**?

Section 4 - The Relationship Between Repentance and Faith

Repentance and faith are distinct yet inseparable. Scripture does not allow for one without the other. Repentance without faith becomes moral reform; faith without repentance becomes presumption.[4]

Repentance turns **from sin**; faith turns **to Christ**. Together, they describe a single movement of the sinner—away from self and toward the Savior. They occur simultaneously, as two aspects of the same Spirit-enabled response to the gospel.

> "Testifying both to Jews and to Greeks of repentance toward God and of faith in our Lord Jesus Christ."
> —Acts 20:21

Reflection & Discussion

1. Why is it dangerous to separate repentance and faith?
2. How do repentance and faith function together in conversion?
3. Do you find yourself emphasizing repentance or faith more? Why might Scripture insist on both?

Section 5 - Salvation Received, Not Earned

The gospel consistently guards against any suggestion that repentance and faith earn salvation. Scripture is explicit that salvation is by grace alone, grounded solely in Christ's finished work.[5]

> "He saved us, not because of works done by us in righteousness, but according to His own mercy."
> —Titus 3:5

Repentance does not cancel guilt; Christ does. Faith does not produce righteousness; Christ provides it. The sinner contributes nothing to salvation except the sin that makes salvation necessary.

This truth preserves assurance. Salvation rests not on the quality of one's repentance or the strength of one's faith, but on the sufficiency of Christ. Weak faith in a strong Savior saves just as surely as strong faith—because salvation depends on Christ, not the believer.

Reflection & Discussion

1. Why do people struggle to accept salvation as entirely unearned?
2. How does this section protect believers from despair and pride?
3. How does this truth reshape assurance?
4. When you fail, do you question Christ's sufficiency—or your worthiness?

Section 6 - The Urgency of the Gospel Call

Because the gospel is true and Christ's work is final, the call to respond is urgent. Scripture never treats the gospel as a matter of indifference or delay.

> "Now is the favorable time; behold, now is the day of salvation."
> —2 Corinthians 6:2

The urgency of the gospel does not arise from emotional pressure or fear-based manipulation, but from reality itself. Life is brief. Judgment is certain. Christ is sufficient. The call to repent and believe is not merely an invitation—it is a moment of divine mercy.

Yet urgency must never be confused with coercion. Scripture calls sinners to respond freely, genuinely, and sincerely—while making clear that salvation itself is the work of God from beginning to end.

Reflection & Discussion

1. Why does Scripture emphasize urgency without coercion?
2. How can urgency be communicated faithfully and compassionately?
3. What dangers arise when the gospel is treated casually?

Section 7 - The Gospel Response Within God's Saving Purpose

While sinners are commanded to repent and believe, Scripture also affirms that those who respond do so because God is at work within them. The call of the gospel does not compete with God's sovereignty—it accomplishes God's purpose.

> "All that the Father gives Me will come to Me."
> —John 6:37

This truth prepares the way for the next stage of our study. If salvation is received through repentance and faith, yet ultimately brought about by God's power and grace, then we must ask how God applies Christ's finished work to individual sinners.

Salvation is not earned by human effort, achieved through religious performance, or secured by decision alone. It is received through repentance and faith—responses enabled by grace and grounded in Christ's finished work. The gospel does not ask sinners to save themselves, but to trust wholly in the Savior God has provided.

Reflection & Discussion

1. How does God's sovereignty give confidence in gospel ministry?
2. Why is this truth comforting rather than discouraging?
3. How does it prepare us for understanding the Spirit's work?

Chapter Summary

Christ has fully accomplished redemption.
Sinners receive that redemption through repentance and faith—responses enabled by grace and grounded in Christ's finished work.

The gospel does not ask sinners to save themselves. It calls them to trust wholly in the Savior God has provided.

Looking Ahead
If salvation is received through repentance and faith, **how does God apply Christ's finished work to the heart of the sinner?**

In the next chapter, we turn to **the saving work of the Holy Spirit and the order of salvation**—how God brings sinners from death to life.

Chapter 5 Endnotes

1. Scripture presents the gospel call as authoritative and universal, grounded in Christ's finished work (Acts 17:30; Mark 1:15).
2. Repentance is a Spirit-enabled turning to God, not a meritorious work (Acts 11:18; 2 Timothy 2:25).
3. Faith is trust in Christ alone and is itself a gift of grace (Ephesians 2:8; Philippians 1:29).
4. Repentance and faith are inseparable aspects of conversion (Acts 20:21).
5. Salvation is received by grace, not earned by obedience or decision (Titus 3:5; Romans 3:24).

CHAPTER 6

THE APPLICATION OF REDEMPTION
THE WORK OF THE HOLY SPIRIT

Chapter Overview

To understand how the salvation accomplished by Christ is **personally applied** to sinners by the Holy Spirit—bringing them from spiritual death to eternal life through a unified and gracious work of God.

Salvation is not only something Christ achieved in history; it is something the Holy Spirit **applies in time**. What the Father planned, and the Son secured, the Spirit now brings to life in the hearts of God's people.

> "No one can say 'Jesus is Lord' except in the Holy Spirit."
> —1 Corinthians 12:3

The Holy Spirit does not add to Christ's finished work, nor does He replace it. He faithfully applies what Christ has already accomplished—awakening dead hearts, uniting believers to Christ, and bringing them into the full enjoyment of salvation. From first awakening to final glorification, salvation is the work of God alone.[1]

Opening Reflection

In the previous session, we saw that Christ's saving work is complete, sufficient, and final. Nothing can be added to it. Nothing remains undone. Yet Scripture also makes clear that salvation must be **personally applied**. No one is saved merely by knowing facts about Jesus or admiring His work from a distance.

This session focuses on **how God brings sinners from death to life**—not through chance, effort, or self-initiation, but through His sovereign and gracious work.

Section 1 — Effectual Calling

God's saving work begins with His effectual call—a powerful, inward summons by which the Holy Spirit brings sinners to life and draws them to Christ.[2]

This calling is more than a general invitation encountered through hearing the gospel; it is the powerful, inward work of the Holy Spirit that brings sinners to life.

> "Those whom He predestined He also called."
> —Romans 8:30

Effectual calling ensures that God's saving purpose is accomplished. This call does not depend on human readiness, wisdom, or merit. Left to themselves, sinners are spiritually deaf to the gospel. When God calls effectually, the Spirit works within the heart, overcoming resistance and enabling a willing response to Christ.

Effectual calling ordinarily takes place through the proclamation of the gospel. As God's Word is preached, the

Spirit works invisibly and powerfully in the hearts of those God has chosen.

> "The Lord opened her heart to pay attention to what was said by Paul."
> —Acts 16:14

This call is life-giving and decisive. It does not coerce, but it transforms. Those whom God calls effectually are brought freely and willingly to Christ because their hearts have been changed. God's call does not force belief—it **creates willingness** by transforming the heart.

Reflection & Discussion

1. Why is an inward call necessary in addition to hearing the gospel?
2. How does effectual calling protect salvation from depending on human ability?

Section 2 - Regeneration: New Life Given

Effectual calling results in regeneration—the sovereign act by which the Holy Spirit imparts new spiritual life to those who were spiritually dead.[3]

Scripture describes this work as being "born again" or "made alive."

> "According to His great mercy, He has caused us to be born again."
> —1 Peter 1:3

Regeneration is not moral improvement, behavioral reform, or religious awakening. It is resurrection. The spiritually dead heart is made alive; blind eyes are opened; hardened resistance is replaced with spiritual responsiveness. Where there was once hostility toward God, there is now desire for Him.

Scripture teaches that, apart from this work of the Spirit, sinners are incapable of responding rightly to God.

> "The natural person does not accept the things of the Spirit of God."
> —1 Corinthians 2:14

Regeneration precedes and produces repentance and faith. Sinners do not regenerate themselves by believing; rather, they believe because they have been made alive. This truth preserves grace and excludes boasting.

> "Even when we were dead… [God] made us alive together with Christ."
> —Ephesians 2:5

Sinners do not believe in order to be born again; they believe **because** they have been made alive.

Reflection & Discussion

1. Why is the image of "new birth" so important?

2. Why must regeneration precede faith?
3. How does this truth safeguard grace from human boasting?

Section 3 - Union with Christ: The Heart of Salvation

Salvation is not merely receiving benefits—it is receiving Christ Himself.

Through regeneration, the Holy Spirit unites the believer to Jesus Christ. **Union with Christ** is the central reality of salvation—the bond by which all saving benefits become ours.

> "You are in Christ Jesus."
> —1 Corinthians 1:30

Salvation is not received as isolated benefits, but as participation in Christ Himself. His death becomes our death to sin. His resurrection becomes our new life. His righteousness becomes our righteousness.

This union is spiritual, real, and unbreakable. It does not collapse human identity, nor does it blur the distinction between Christ and the believer. Rather, it establishes a living relationship secured by the Spirit and grounded in grace.

Reflection & Discussion

1. Why is union with Christ central to salvation?
2. How does this shape our understanding of Christian identity?

Section 4 – Justification

Flowing from union with Christ, God justifies the sinner—declaring them righteous in His sight on the basis of Christ's righteousness alone.[4]

> "Therefore, since we have been justified by faith, we have peace with God."
> —Romans 5:1

Justification is a forensic, **legal declaration**, not a moral process.[4] God does not make sinners righteous in justification; He **declares** them righteous by crediting Christ's obedience to them. At the same time, the sinner's guilt is fully forgiven.

Scripture uses courtroom language to describe justification because it answers a legal question: *How can a holy God declare a guilty sinner righteous without compromising His justice?* In justification, God acts as Judge, not physician. He does not first make the sinner morally righteous and then declare them justified; He declares them righteous because Christ's obedience and atoning death have fully satisfied the law on their behalf. Though sin still remains in the believer's life, it no longer defines their standing before God. The verdict has already been rendered. Justification changes a sinner's status, not their nature—and that unchanging verdict becomes the foundation upon which all growth in holiness rests.

This declaration occurs once, completely, and forever. It is not repeated, reversed, or diminished. The believer's standing before God rests entirely on what Christ has done, not on ongoing performance.

Reflection & Discussion

1. Why must justification be forensic rather than progressive?
2. How does justification provide assurance?

Section 5 - Adoption

Having been declared righteous through justification, believers are also welcomed into God's family through adoption. Salvation brings not only forgiveness but belonging.[5]

> "You have received the Spirit of adoption as sons."
> —Romans 8:15

Adoption is God's gracious act of receiving justified sinners into His household as beloved children. Adoption moves beyond forgiveness to belonging. Believers are no longer enemies or servants, but beloved children with full family privileges.

Through adoption, believers receive:

- a new status — children of God
- a new family — united with other believers
- a new inheritance — heirs of eternal life
- a new assurance — the Spirit testifying to God's fatherly love

Adoption reshapes how believers relate to God—not merely as Judge, but as Father—and transforms obedience from fearful duty into grateful love.

Reflection & Discussion

1. How does adoption reshape how we relate to God?
2. Why is adoption essential to assurance?

Section 6 – Sanctification

Those whom God justifies and adopts; He also sanctifies. While justification is a once-for-all declaration, sanctification is the lifelong work of the Spirit by which believers are progressively conformed to the image of Christ.[6]

> "For this is the will of God, your sanctification."
> —1 Thessalonians 4:3

Sanctification refers both to being set apart for God at salvation and to the ongoing process by which believers grow in holiness. The Holy Spirit works within believers to convict us of sin, to renew our minds, and to produce Christlike character.

Sanctification is the fruit of salvation, not the root. Holiness does not earn acceptance with God; it flows from it. Though believers continue to battle sin in this life, sin no longer reigns. Growth is real, continual, and Grace-driven.

Reflection & Discussion

1. Why must sanctification never be confused with justification?
2. How does grace fuel growth rather than undermine it?

Section 7 - Perseverance

Those whom God saves; He also keeps.[7] Scripture teaches that all who are truly regenerated and justified will be preserved by God and will persevere in faith until the end.[7]

> "He who began a good work in you will bring it to completion."
> —Philippians 1:6

Perseverance does not mean believers live flawlessly or never struggle. It means God will not abandon His people or allow them to finally fall away. Their perseverance rests not on personal strength, but on God's faithfulness, Christ's finished work, and the sealing ministry of the Spirit.

> "No one will snatch them out of My hand."
> —John 10:28

True believers may wander, stumble, and experience seasons of weakness—but God's preserving grace ensures their faith endures.

Reflection & Discussion

1. How does perseverance protect assurance?

2. Why does this doctrine encourage humility rather than complacency?

Section 8 - Glorification

The application of redemption culminates in glorification—the final transformation of believers into perfect conformity with Christ.[8]

> "If the Spirit of Him who raised Jesus from the dead dwells in you, He… will also give life to your mortal bodies."
> —Romans 8:11

Glorification is freedom from sin, death, suffering, and corruption forever. Believers will be raised in glory, transformed fully, and brought into everlasting communion with God. Salvation will be complete—body and soul—forever with Christ.

The same Spirit who calls, regenerates, unites, justifies, adopts, sanctifies, and preserves God's people will also glorify them. Salvation from start to finish is the work of God alone.

From first awakening to final assurance, every stage of salvation is the gracious work of the Holy Spirit, faithfully applying the finished work of Christ and bringing God's people from death to life.

Reflection & Discussion

1. Why must salvation include bodily resurrection?
2. How does future glory shape present faithfulness?

Chapter Summary

Salvation is not a human achievement but a divine rescue. What Christ accomplished in history; the Spirit brings to life in the believer.

God brings His people from death to life through a gracious, purposeful order—calling, regenerating, granting faith, justifying, adopting, sanctifying, preserving, and glorifying them. This truth grounds assurance, humbles pride, and magnifies grace.

Closing Reflection

How does understanding the Spirit's work deepen your assurance and gratitude toward God?

Preparation for Next Chapter

In the next Chapter, we will address a deeply personal question:

How can I know that I am truly saved—and how does God preserve His people to the end?

We will examine assurance, perseverance, and the promises that secure the believer's hope.

Chapter 6 Endnotes

1. The salvation applied by the Spirit flows from Christ's finished work and fulfills the Father's eternal purpose (John 16:14; Rom. 8:30).
2. Effectual calling describes the Spirit's inward work accompanying the preached Word (Rom. 8:30; Acts 16:14).
3. Regeneration is God's sovereign act of giving life to the spiritually dead (John 3:3–8; 1 Cor. 2:14).
4. Justification is a once-for-all legal declaration grounded in Christ's righteousness (Rom. 5:1; 2 Cor. 5:21).
5. Adoption brings believers into God's family with full rights and assurance (Rom. 8:15–17; Gal. 4:4–7).
6. Sanctification is the ongoing work of the Spirit producing holiness in believers (1 Thess. 4:3; Gal. 5:22–23).
7. Perseverance rests on God's preserving grace, not human effort (Phil. 1:6; John 10:28–29).
8. Glorification completes salvation with resurrection and eternal life (Rom. 8:11; 1 John 3:2).

CHAPTER 7

THE ORDER OF SALVATION (ORDO SALUTIS)

FROM CALLING TO GLORY

Chapter Overview

Salvation is not merely something God does *to* sinners—it is a new life He brings them *into*. While Scripture teaches that salvation is accomplished by Christ and applied by the Holy Spirit according to God's sovereign purpose, it also teaches that this salvation unfolds in the real lives of real people over time. That means it is not abstract. It is personal. It is about you and me.

God has rescued us from sin, eternal death, and divine judgment—and He has brought us into a life that is now being shaped by His grace.

> "And we know that for those who love God all things work together for good, for those who are called according to His purpose."
> —Romans 8:28

The Bible speaks of salvation as a unified work of grace with a clear order and direction.[1]

This order—often called the *ordo salutis*—is not given to satisfy theological curiosity, but to help believers understand what

God has done, what He is doing, and what He will surely complete.

Understanding the order of salvation guards the gospel from confusion. It prevents us from reversing cause and effect—such as making faith the source of regeneration rather than its result. It protects grace from being diluted into human decisionism. And it anchors assurance not in our performance, but in God's faithful and sovereign work.

Most importantly, the order of salvation directs attention away from ourselves and back to God. Each step originates in His will, is carried out by His power, and exists for His glory. From first awakening to final glory, salvation is wholly the work of God's grace.

This chapter revisits the gracious work described in the previous chapter, but from a different perspective. Here, we consider not the *foundation* of salvation, but its *outworking*—not as the ground of assurance, but as the fruit of God's saving work in the life of the believer.

Section 1 - God's Eternal Purpose — A Salvation That Was Not an Accident

Before salvation enters the realm of time, its origin lies in eternity. Scripture teaches that God's saving purpose was established before the foundation of the world.[2]

Salvation does not begin with human seeking, but with God's gracious and sovereign intention to redeem a people for Himself.

> "He chose us in Him before the foundation of the world." —Ephesians 1:4

Long before a believer ever heard the gospel, felt conviction, or responded in faith, God had already set His saving purpose in motion.

Scripture teaches that salvation originates in God's eternal will, not human initiative. This truth does not invite speculation—it provides comfort. Believers do not discover that their salvation rests on a fragile decision or fluctuating commitment, but on God's unchanging purpose.

> "For I know the plans I have for you, declares the LORD, plans for welfare and not for evil, to give you a future and a hope." — Jeremiah 29:11

This promise, originally given to God's people in exile, reflects a broader biblical truth: God's purposes toward His people are never random or cruel, but intentional and redemptive.

For many believers, this becomes clear only in hindsight. Looking back, believers often recognize that God was at work long before they were aware of it—placing people in their lives, exposing false assurances, allowing dissatisfaction with sin, or awakening questions that would not go away. Salvation was not a coincidence.

> "For it is God who works in you, both to will and to work for his good pleasure." —Philippians 2:13

This was the quiet, intentional work of the Holy Spirit, carrying out a purpose God had already set in motion.

Reflection & Discussion

1. When you look back, where do you see God working in your life before you responded to Him?
2. How does knowing that salvation began with God—not you—affect assurance?
3. Why is God's eternal purpose a comfort rather than a threat to faith?

Section 2 - Effectual Calling — When the Gospel Became Personal

At some point, God's eternal purpose breaks into a person's life through His effectual call.[3]

It is at this time that the Holy Spirit convinces sinners of their sin, enlightens their minds to see Christ's work, and renews their wills, enabling them to freely embrace Jesus for salvation.

> "who saved us and called us to a holy calling, not because of our works but because of his own purpose and grace, which he gave us in Christ Jesus before the ages began,"
> —2 Timothy 1:9

For some, this call came through a sermon, a conversation, a Bible verse, or a season of crisis. For others, it unfolded gradually through persistent conviction and growing unease with sin. The outward circumstances may differ, but the inward reality is the same: God made the gospel impossible to ignore.

Effectual calling does not always feel dramatic. Sometimes it is quiet, unsettling, and persistent. What marks it is not emotion, but clarity—a growing awareness that God is addressing *you*, not people in general.

The gospel stops being information and becomes confrontational.

This call does not force belief, but it awakens the heart so that belief becomes possible. This is the Holy Spirit tugging at your heart. This is God calling us into saving union with His Son—a real, personal, transforming relationship grounded in truth and grace.

Reflection & Discussion

1. What circumstances surrounded your awareness that God was personally calling you?
2. How did the gospel move from "true" to "urgent"?
3. Why is this call described as effectual rather than merely invitational?

Section 3 - Regeneration — From Death to Life

Before regeneration, sinners are not merely confused or misguided—they are spiritually dead. When God transforms a person, He does not reform the old heart; He gives a new one.

Scripture calls this work regeneration—the Holy Spirit's supernatural act of giving spiritual life to the dead sinner, making them a "new creation" or "born again" so they can believe in Christ.[4]

This is a profound inner transformation described as a new birth, spiritual awakening, and divine renewal, distinct from physical birth but just as miraculous. It's God's work alone, enabling new desires for God, leading to faith, repentance, and a new way of living.

This new birth may not be immediately recognized. Jesus explained to the Pharisee Nicodemus that being "born again" is not a physical return to the womb, but a supernatural work of God—a spiritual rebirth accomplished by the Holy Spirit (John 3:3–8).

Paul describes this same reality as becoming "a new creation in Christ," a decisive change in which the old life passes away, and new life begins (2 Corinthians 5:17).

Regeneration is therefore not self-produced or gradually achieved. It is the sovereign work of God—cleansing the sinner, imparting new life, and creating a heart capable of faith and repentance. It is accomplished by the same divine power that raised Christ from the dead, and it is received entirely by grace, not earned through human effort.

When regeneration occurs, something fundamentally changes. The person is no longer who they were. The old life has passed away, and a new life has begun. They now see with:

- a new awareness of sin
- a new sensitivity to God's Word
- a new desire for holiness
- a new longing for Christ

Reflection & Discussion

- What changes did you notice after God brought you to life?
- Why must regeneration precede repentance and faith?
- How does this protect salvation from becoming self-produced?

Section 4 - Repentance and Faith — Turning and Trusting

Repentance and faith are the Spirit-enabled responses that flow from new life in Christ.[5]

They are not human contributions to salvation, but the visible expression of a heart that has already been made alive by God. Scripture consistently presents repentance and faith as inseparable—two aspects of the same saving response: turning from sin and trusting in Christ.

As we saw in Chapter 5, repentance and faith are distinct yet inseparable graces. Faith turns toward Christ in trusting dependence; repentance turns away from sin in responsive submission. In the order of salvation, these do not precede regeneration as its cause but follow regeneration as its necessary fruit.

It is important that we understand that faith is not mere agreement with facts. Head knowledge about God, Scripture, or even the historical events of Jesus' life is not saving faith. One can acknowledge biblical truth without surrendering to Christ.

Scripture makes this distinction unmistakably clear. Even the demons recognize who Jesus is and acknowledge His authority.

> "You believe that God is one; you do well. Even the demons believe—and shudder!"
> —James 2:19

The demons knew Jesus' identity. They feared His authority. Yet they were not redeemed. Knowledge alone does not save.

Saving faith reaches beyond belief about God; and becomes trust in God. It is personal reliance upon Jesus Christ—resting wholly in His person and His finished work. Faith abandons all confidence in self-effort, morality, or religious performance and clings to Christ alone.

Faith receives Jesus not only as Savior, but as Lord. It is not merely intellectual assent; it is relational trust. Believers do not simply know facts about Christ—they know Christ Himself. Repentance is the necessary companion of faith. It is not mere regret over consequences, nor temporary sorrow over being caught. Repentance is a decisive turning—a change of mind and heart about sin and about God.

The believer begins to see sin as God sees it: not as freedom, but as bondage; not as harmless, but as destructive. Repentance involves dying to self, renouncing former loyalties, and turning toward God with a renewed heart.

> "Repent therefore, and turn back, that your sins may be blotted out."
> —Acts 3:19

While repentance begins at conversion, it does not end there. It becomes a pattern of the Christian life. As believers grow, they continue to turn away from sin and toward God—confessing, forsaking, and walking in new obedience. This ongoing repentance is not evidence of failure, but of life.

Together, repentance and faith mark the believer's entrance into conscious fellowship with Christ. They do not earn salvation; they receive it. They are not the root of new life, but its fruit.

In essence, the new life God has given becomes the source from which trusting Christ (faith) and turning from sin (repentance) continually flow. This is how salvation is lived—

by grace, through faith, in ongoing repentance—resulting in freedom, new purpose, and growing Christlikeness.

Reflection & Discussion

- How is biblical faith different from intellectual belief?
- In what ways has repentance continued since your conversion?
- Why must repentance and faith always remain connected?

Section 5 - Justification — Living as One Declared Righteous

Justification answers one of the believer's deepest questions: *How do I now stand before God?*

Justification is the moment God declares a sinner righteous in His sight—not because of anything the sinner has done, but because of everything Christ has done.[6] It is not a process of becoming righteous, but a once-for-all verdict issued by God Himself.

> "Therefore, since we have been justified by faith, we have peace with God through our Lord Jesus Christ."
> —Romans 5:1

While justification is a legal declaration in heaven, it produces very real effects on earth. Many believers first experience justification not as a theological category, but as a profound change in their standing before God. The crushing weight of guilt lifts. Fear of condemnation gives way to peace. The relationship with God changes from distance to nearness.

Before justification, even sincere religious people often live with an underlying uncertainty. They hope God will accept them. They try to balance their failures with good intentions. They fear judgment, even if they rarely speak of it. After justification, something shifts: the believer no longer relates to God as a condemned sinner hoping for mercy, but as a forgiven sinner resting in grace.

Justification answers the question:
"How can a holy God accept a guilty sinner?"
The answer is not found in personal improvement, moral resolve, or religious effort. It is found entirely in Christ's righteousness credited to the believer.

> "For our sake He made Him to be sin who knew no sin, so that in Him we might become the righteousness of God."
> —2 Corinthians 5:21

This means that when God looks upon the justified believer, He does not see lingering guilt or partial righteousness. He sees the perfect obedience of His Son. The believer stands before God fully forgiven, fully accepted, and fully secure—not because of spiritual progress, but because of Christ's finished work.

Justification also reshapes how believers live. It removes the exhausting effort to earn God's approval. Obedience no longer flows from fear of rejection, but from gratitude for acceptance.

The believer does not pursue holiness to become justified, but because they already are.

Perhaps most importantly, justification anchors assurance. The believer's confidence rests not in the strength of repentance, the consistency of faith, or the visible progress of sanctification, but in the unchanging verdict God has already declared.

> "There is therefore now no condemnation for those who are in Christ Jesus."
> —Romans 8:1

Justification means:

- The case is closed.
- The verdict is final.
- The record is cleared.
- The sinner is declared righteous—forever.

Justification changes our standing before God—but it also opens the door to a new relationship. God does not merely forgive and release sinners; He welcomes them into His family.

This leads us to the next blessing of salvation:
Adoption — living as children of God.

Reflection & Discussion

- How does justification affect the way you handle guilt?
- Why is justification foundational to assurance?

- What happens when believers confuse justification with sanctification?

Section 6 - Adoption — Living as God's Child

Justification changes a believer's standing before God. Adoption changes their relationship with Him.

When God saves a sinner, He does more than forgive them—He brings them into His family.[7]

> "You have received the Spirit of adoption as sons, by whom we cry, 'Abba! Father!'"
> —Romans 8:15

Adoption means that believers are no longer spiritual outsiders, servants hoping to earn favor, or strangers approaching God at a distance. They are sons and daughters—fully welcomed, fully loved, and permanently belonging to God.

This new identity reshapes how believers understand themselves and their lives.

- You are no longer defined by your past, but by your Father
- You are no longer striving to belong—you already do
- You are no longer living for approval—you are already loved

Adoption also brings assurance. God does not adopt reluctantly or temporarily. He does not revoke His fatherly care when His children stumble. Discipline may come, but abandonment never will.

> "For the Lord disciplines the one He loves, and chastises every son whom He receives."
> —Hebrews 12:6

The Spirit confirms this identity internally. Believers find themselves drawn to God—not merely out of duty, but with affection. Prayer becomes relational rather than transactional. Obedience becomes an expression of love rather than fear. Adoption also carries responsibility. Children of God are called to reflect their Father's character. They represent Him in the world as ambassadors of grace, truth, and reconciliation. Their lives become a testimony—not of perfection, but of belonging. Believers are also heirs.

> "If children, then heirs—heirs of God and fellow heirs with Christ."
> —Romans 8:17

This inheritance is not merely future glory, but present security. God's promises belong to His children. His presence accompanies them. His purposes govern their lives.

To live as an adopted child of God is to walk with confidence, humility, and hope—knowing that salvation has not merely changed your destination, but your identity.

You are no longer a slave.
You are no longer an orphan.
You are a child of God.

Reflection & Discussion

1. How does adoption reshape your identity?
2. What fears does adoption remove?
3. How does being God's child affect obedience?

Section 7 - Sanctification — Growing in Newness of Life

Those whom God justifies and adopts; He also sanctifies. Sanctification is the lifelong process by which believers are progressively conformed to the image of Christ.[8]

> "For this is the will of God, your sanctification."
> —1 Thessalonians 4:3

Unlike justification, which happens once and for all, sanctification unfolds over time. It is the ongoing work of God in the believer's life by which sin is increasingly put to death and obedience increasingly takes shape. While believers are fully accepted in Christ, they are not yet fully perfected. Sanctification describes the daily outworking of the new life God has already given.

A Life Set Apart to God

Sanctification means being *set apart* for God. At conversion, believers are set apart decisively as God's own, and from that point forward, they grow progressively into the likeness of Christ. Scripture speaks of this dual reality:

> "You are in Christ Jesus, who became to us wisdom from God, righteousness and sanctification and redemption."
> —1 Corinthians 1:30

In Christ, believers already belong to God. They are no longer under sin's dominion. Yet they are also being shaped, trained, and transformed over time. Sanctification is both a position we have in Christ and a process we experience in daily life.

The Ongoing Battle with Sin

Although sin no longer reigns, it still resists. The Christian life involves real struggle. Believers continue to face temptation, weakness, and failure—but no longer as slaves. Sin is now something to be resisted, confessed, and fought by the power of the Holy Spirit.

Sanctification does not mean instant moral perfection. It means a new direction in life. Where once sin was embraced, it is now opposed. Where once God was ignored, He is now sought. Where once self-ruled, Christ now reigns.

This battle is evidence of life, not failure. Dead people do not struggle. Only living people do.

What Sanctification Looks Like in Everyday Life

Sanctification is not abstract or mystical. It shows up in ordinary, daily obedience shaped by grace. It includes:

- Growing hatred for sin and love for holiness
- A deeper desire for God and His Word
- Increasing humility and dependence on grace
- Learning to forgive rather than hold bitterness
- Choosing truth over deceit
- Growing self-control in areas like speech, sexuality, and finances
- Enduring hardship with trust rather than despair
- Obedience even when it is costly or unseen

These changes do not happen all at once. Growth is often uneven. Some seasons feel fruitful; others feel slow or painful. But over time, there is movement — a direction toward Christlikeness.

God's Work and Our Participation

Sanctification is both God's work and our lived experience. The Holy Spirit convicts, renews, strengthens, and transforms. At the same time, believers are called to actively pursue obedience.

Scripture holds these truths together without contradiction. God works in us, and we respond by walking in obedience. We do not sanctify ourselves apart from God, but neither are we passive. We cooperate with grace through prayer, Scripture, fellowship, repentance, and perseverance.

Growth happens not through self-effort alone, but through dependence on the Spirit who indwells us.

Progress, Not Perfection

Sanctification should not be measured by perfection but by direction. A believer may stumble, but they do not settle. They may fall, but they return to Christ. Over time, there is an increasing desire to please God, a deeper sorrow over sin, and a growing love for righteousness.

This process strengthens assurance. The presence of spiritual fruit—even imperfectly expressed—is evidence that God is at work.

> "He who began a good work in you will bring it to completion at the day of Jesus Christ."
> —Philippians 1:6

Believers are not yet what they will be, but they are no longer what they once were. God is actively shaping His children for the glory that awaits.

Reflection & Discussion

1. Where have you seen growth—and struggle—in sanctification?
2. Why does God use time rather than instant perfection?
3. How does sanctification strengthen assurance?

Section 8 - Perseverance — Held Fast Through Trials

Those whom God saves, He also preserves.[9]

Perseverance is not the believer's stubborn effort to hold on to God, but God's faithful commitment to hold on to His people. The same grace that calls, regenerates, justifies, and adopts also sustains believers through every season of life until the end. Jesus Himself promised this security:

> "My sheep hear my voice, and I know them, and they follow me. I give them eternal life, and they will never perish, and no one will snatch them out of my hand."
> —John 10:27–28

Perseverance means that true believers continue in faith—not perfectly, but genuinely. They may stumble, struggle, and suffer, yet they do not finally fall away. God preserves them, and that preserving grace expresses itself in a persevering faith.

Perseverance Is God's Work Before It Is Ours

Scripture consistently teaches that perseverance rests on God's faithfulness, not human strength.

> "He who began a good work in you will bring it to completion at the day of Jesus Christ."
> —Philippians 1:6

Believers persevere because God is at work within them. The same Spirit who gave new life continues to sustain that life. Perseverance is not maintained by willpower alone, emotional consistency, or flawless obedience. It is maintained by God's unchanging purpose, Christ's finished work, and the Spirit's ongoing ministry.

This truth brings deep comfort. Salvation does not rest on how tightly we hold onto Christ, but on how firmly He holds onto us.

Perseverance Is Experienced Through Real Life

Perseverance does not mean an easy or uninterrupted spiritual journey. Scripture never promises a trouble-free life. In fact, believers are told to expect trials, suffering, and discipline.

> "Through many tribulations we must enter the kingdom of God."
> —Acts 14:22

Faith is refined through hardship. Trials expose what we truly trust and deepen our dependence on God. Seasons of suffering, doubt, weakness, or dryness do not mean salvation has failed. Often, they become the very means God uses to strengthen faith, humble the heart, and draw believers closer to Himself.

Perseverance looks like returning to Christ even when the heart feels weary. It looks like continuing to pray when prayers feel weak, continuing to confess sin rather than hide it, and continuing to cling to God's promises when emotions waver.

Perseverance Is Not Perfection

Believers still sin. They still struggle. They may stumble seriously at times. But perseverance means they do not remain comfortable in sin or abandon Christ altogether.

When a believer falls, the Holy Spirit convicts, corrects, and restores. God disciplines His children not to condemn them, but to heal and mature them.

> "For the Lord disciplines the one he loves, and chastises every son whom he receives."
> —Hebrews 12:6

Perseverance is marked by repentance, not perfection. A persevering believer may fall, but they do not settle into rebellion. They may wander, but they are drawn back. They may struggle, but they do not stop believing.

Perseverance Bears Fruit Over Time

One of the clearest evidences of perseverance is growth—slow, uneven, often quiet growth, but real growth nonetheless.

Over time, the believer increasingly displays:

- A deeper love for Christ
- A growing hatred of sin
- A desire to obey God
- Humility and teachability
- Endurance through hardship

- A longing for holiness
- Love for God's people
- Hope in future glory

These are not achieved overnight. They develop through years of walking with God. Perseverance is not dramatic consistency but faithful continuation.

Jesus described this endurance when He said:

> "The one who endures to the end will be saved."
> —Matthew 24:13

This does not mean endurance earns salvation, but that endurance proves salvation is real.

Perseverance and Assurance

Understanding perseverance strengthens assurance rather than undermines it. Believers do not live in constant fear of losing salvation. Instead, they rest in the promise that God finishes what He starts.

When doubts arise, believers are invited not to look inward for perfection but outward to Christ's faithfulness. Assurance grows as we see God sustaining our faith through trials, correcting us when we wander, and continually drawing us back to Himself.

Perseverance teaches us to say with confidence:

> "The Lord will rescue me from every evil deed and bring me safely into his heavenly kingdom."
> —2 Timothy 4:18

Perseverance Points Us Toward Glory

Perseverance is not the end of the story—it leads to glorification. God's purpose is not merely to help believers survive this life, but to bring them safely home.

One day, the struggle with sin will end.
Faith will give way to sight.
Hope will be fulfilled.
Suffering will cease.

Those who persevere by God's grace will be fully transformed into the likeness of Christ.

> "Those whom he justified he also glorified."
> —Romans 8:30

The chain is unbroken. What God begins, He completes.

Perseverance is the lived expression of saving faith over time. It is not self-reliance, but God's preserving grace at work in the believer's life. Though the Christian path includes hardship, discipline, and struggle, it is upheld by divine faithfulness from beginning to end.

Believers persevere because God preserves.
They endure because Christ intercedes.
They continue because the Spirit sustains.
And in the end, they will stand—not because they were strong, but because God was faithful.

Reflection & Discussion

1. How does perseverance differ from mere endurance?
2. What sustains believers during suffering?
3. Why does perseverance matter for assurance?

Section 9 - Glorification (Hope Fulfilled)

Glorification is the final and certain completion of God's saving work.[10] What God purposed in eternity, accomplished in Christ, applied by the Spirit, and sustained through perseverance, will one day be brought to perfect fulfillment.

> "For those whom He justified He also glorified."
> —Romans 8:30

Notice the certainty of Paul's language. Glorification is spoken of in the past tense, not because it has already occurred, but because, in God's saving purpose, it is guaranteed. Not one whom God saves will fail to reach this final glory.

Glorification is the moment when sin is completely removed, suffering ends forever, and believers are made to be fully like

Christ. What sanctification has been imperfectly shaped will then be perfected entirely.

> "Beloved, we are God's children now, and what we will be has not yet appeared; but we know that when He appears we shall be like Him, because we shall see Him as He is."
> —1 John 3:2

What Glorification Means

Glorification includes the resurrection of the body, the complete freedom from sin, and the full enjoyment of God's presence forever.

This is not the escape of the soul from the body, but the redemption of the whole person. Just as Christ was raised bodily in glory, so too will believers be raised with imperishable, transformed bodies.

> "So also is the resurrection of the dead. What is sown is perishable; what is raised is imperishable."
> —1 Corinthians 15:42

In glorification:

- Sin will no longer tempt, deceive, or accuse.
- Weakness, sickness, and death will be gone.
- Faith will give way to sight.
- Hope will give way to fulfillment.
- The battle will be over.

Hope That Shapes the Present

Glorification is not merely a future promise—it is a present anchor. The certainty of future glory strengthens believers to endure present suffering.

> "For I consider that the sufferings of this present time are not worth comparing with the glory that is to be revealed to us."—Romans 8:18

Suffering does not mean God has abandoned His people. Difficulty does not signal failure in salvation. Trials are not detours from God's plan—they are part of the road that leads to glory.

For the believer, pain is temporary. Glory is eternal.

This hope does not minimize suffering, but it gives it meaning. It reminds believers that no hardship, loss, or sorrow has the final word.

Life in the Presence of God

Glorification culminates not merely in personal perfection but in eternal communion with God.

> "Behold, the dwelling place of God is with man. He will dwell with them, and they will be His people."
> —Revelation 21:3

This is the fulfillment of every promise:

- God with His people
- Sin fully removed
- Creation restored
- Joy unbroken

The story that began in a garden and was fractured by sin ends in a renewed creation where righteousness dwells and Christ reigns forever.

Assurance Completed

Glorification completes the believer's assurance. What began with calling and regeneration ends with eternal life in God's presence.

The believer's hope does not rest in personal faithfulness, strength, or endurance—but in God's faithfulness to finish what He started.

> "He who began a good work in you will bring it to completion at the day of Jesus Christ."
> —Philippians 1:6

The Christian journey does not end in uncertainty. It ends in glory.

Living in Light of Glory

Because glorification is certain, believers are called to live now with an eternal perspective.

This hope:

- Encourages perseverance in suffering
- Produces patience in trials
- Fuels holiness in daily life
- Anchors the soul in confidence

The Christian life is not a march toward exhaustion—it is a pilgrimage toward glory.

Glorification is the promised end of salvation—the day when God's work is complete, sin is gone, and believers are fully transformed into Christ's likeness. It is not wishful thinking, but guaranteed hope grounded in God's faithfulness. The Christian story ends not in struggle, but in glory.

Salvation begins with God.
It unfolds by God's power.
And it ends in God's glory.

Reflection & Discussion

1. How does future glory shape present faithfulness?
2. Why must glorification remain part of the gospel?
3. How does hope sustain perseverance?

Chapter Summary

From Calling to Glory — Living the Salvation God Has Given

This chapter has traced the gracious work of God as it unfolds in the life of every believer. Salvation is not a single moment isolated in the past, nor merely a future hope—it is a living reality that God brings to completion through every season of life.

We began by seeing that salvation originates in God's eternal purpose, not human initiative. Long before we were aware of our need, God was at work, drawing us to Himself according to His gracious plan.

We then considered effectual calling, when the gospel became personal—when God's voice cut through the noise of life and awakened our hearts to Christ. This call was not coercive, but life-giving, making us willing and able to respond.

Next, we reflected on regeneration, the miracle of new birth. God did not merely improve us or reform our behavior; He made us new. We were brought from spiritual death to life, given new desires, new affections, and a new direction.

From that new life flows repentance and faith—not as works that earn salvation, but as the Spirit-enabled responses of a changed heart. We turn from sin and turn to Christ, trusting Him personally and continually as Savior and Lord.

We then explored justification, the gracious declaration that believers are fully forgiven and counted righteous before God through faith in Christ alone. Our standing before God rests not on performance, but on Christ's finished work.

From justification flows adoption, the gift of a new identity. Believers are not merely pardoned criminals; they are beloved children of God, welcomed into His family, given His name, His care, and an eternal inheritance.

We considered sanctification, the ongoing work by which God shapes His children into the likeness of Christ. Though imperfect and often slow, this process reveals real growth—new desires, new obedience, and increasing love for God and others.

We then reflected on perseverance, the assurance that those whom God saves, He sustains. True believers endure not because of their strength, but because God preserves them through faith, even amid trials, suffering, and weakness.

Finally, we lifted our eyes to glorification, the certain hope that one day God will complete His saving work. Every trace of sin will be removed. Our bodies will be raised and renewed. We will dwell forever with Christ in glory, fully restored and forever secure.

Taken together, these truths form a beautiful and comforting picture:

- Salvation begins with God
- Salvation is carried forward by God
- Salvation is completed by God

From calling to glory, salvation is God's work—applied personally, lived daily, and secured eternally.

Chapter 7 Endnotes

1. Romans 8:29–30 presents salvation as a unified, God-initiated sequence culminating in glory.
2. Scripture speaks of God's choosing grace briefly and reverently, emphasizing comfort rather than speculation (Eph. 1:4–5).
3. Effectual calling describes the Spirit's inward work accompanying the gospel (Rom. 8:30; Acts 16:14).
4. Regeneration precedes faith as the Spirit gives life to the dead heart (John 3:3–8; 1 Cor. 2:14).
5. Repentance and faith are Spirit-enabled responses flowing from new life (Acts 11:18; Eph. 2:8).
6. Justification is God's legal declaration grounded in Christ's righteousness (Rom. 5:1; 2 Cor. 5:21).
7. Adoption brings believers into God's family with full assurance (Rom. 8:15–17).
8. Sanctification is the ongoing work of God by which believers are progressively conformed to Christ, flowing from justification and adoption (1 Thess. 4:3; Rom. 6:22).
9. Perseverance rests on God's preserving power, not human strength (John 10:28–29).
10. Glorification completes salvation with resurrection life and eternal communion with God (Rom. 8:30; 1 John 3:2).

CHAPTER 8

THE CHRISTIAN LIFE
Living Out the New Creation

Chapter Overview

Salvation does not terminate with justification, nor does it exist merely as a future hope. Scripture teaches that those who have been united to Christ are made new in the present. Salvation does not merely change our destination—it changes our identity. Scripture teaches that those who are in Christ are not improved versions of their former selves; they are new creations.

> "Therefore, if anyone is in Christ, he is a new creation. The old has passed away; behold, the new has come."
> —2 Corinthians 5:17

The gospel not only rescues sinners from judgment—it transforms how they live. The Christian life flows from salvation and displays it. Because believers have been regenerated, justified, adopted, and indwelt by the Holy Spirit, their lives necessarily begin to reflect this new reality.

This chapter considers how new life in Christ is expressed in ordinary human relationships and in daily faithfulness. Scripture presents Christian living not as a list of rules to follow, but as a transformed way of life empowered by grace, guided by God's Word, and sustained by the Spirit.

Section 1 - Living as New Creations

The Christian life begins with identity, not activity. Scripture consistently grounds obedience in who believers already are in Christ.[1]

> "You have been raised with Christ… For you have died, and your life is hidden with Christ in God."
> —Colossians 3:1–3

To be a new creation means that the believer's fundamental relationship to God, sin, and self has been transformed. The old life—marked by rebellion, self-rule, and spiritual death—has passed away. A new life—marked by reconciliation, submission to Christ, and spiritual vitality—has begun.

This does not mean believers no longer struggle with sin or weakness. It means they now live from a **new identity**. They are no longer defined by who they were in Adam, but by who they are in Christ.

Living as a new creation involves learning to see yourself as God sees you—forgiven, justified, adopted, and made alive. The Christian life begins with embracing this new identity, not striving to earn it.

When God saves a sinner, He does not merely forgive them—He recreates them. Believers are not improved versions of their old selves; they are new creations in Christ.

This new identity affects:

- How we see ourselves
- How we relate to sin
- How we respond to God
- How we live among others

Paul reminds believers that their old identity no longer defines them:

> "You are not your own, for you were bought with a price."
> —1 Corinthians 6:19–20

This new identity produces new desires. Those who have been made alive by the Spirit now long to please God, not to earn His favor, but because they belong to Him. Obedience becomes a response of gratitude rather than a means of acceptance.

The Christian life flows from **who you are**, not who you are trying to become.

Reflection & Discussion

1. Why is identity foundational to Christian living?
2. How does seeing yourself as a "new creation" change how you approach obedience?
3. In what ways do believers sometimes continue living as if the "old life" still defines them?
4. Where are you tempted to live out of your old identity?

Section 2 - Walking by the Spirit

The Christian life is not lived by self-effort, willpower, or religious discipline alone. It is lived by walking in daily dependence upon the Holy Spirit.[2]

> "So I say, walk by the Spirit, and you will not gratify the desires of the flesh."
> —Galatians 5:16

To "walk by the Spirit" means to live under His guidance, strength, and influence rather than being driven by the old sinful nature. This does not mean temptation disappears or that believers no longer struggle with sin. It means that sin no longer rules.

Before Christ, the desires of the flesh dominated the heart. After a new birth, those desires remain—but they are no longer in control. The Spirit empowers believers to resist sin, choose obedience, and grow in Christlikeness.

Walking by the Spirit is not a single decision, but a daily posture of dependence—listening to God's Word, responding to conviction, and yielding one step at a time.

The Fruit of the Spirit: What New Life Looks Like

When believers walk by the Spirit, He produces fruit in their lives—not instantly, not perfectly, but genuinely.

> "But the fruit of the Spirit is love, joy, peace, patience, kindness, goodness, faithfulness, gentleness, self-control."
> —Galatians 5:22–23

This fruit is not manufactured by effort; it is grown by abiding.

What this looks like in everyday life:

- **Love** – choosing sacrificial care for others, even when it is inconvenient
- **Joy** – a settled gladness rooted in Christ, not circumstances
- **Peace** – confidence in God's care, even amid uncertainty or conflict
- **Patience** – enduring frustration without resentment
- **Kindness** – active compassion toward others
- **Goodness** – integrity and moral beauty shaped by God's truth
- **Faithfulness** – reliability, loyalty, and perseverance
- **Gentleness** – strength exercised with humility and care
- **Self-control** – Spirit-enabled restraint rather than flesh-driven impulse

This fruit does not grow overnight. It develops over time as believers continue to walk with Christ, respond to the Spirit's leading, and put sin to death.

What "Not Gratifying the Flesh" Really Means

Galatians 5:16 does not promise a struggle-free life. It promises a **Spirit-governed life**.

The flesh still speaks. Temptation still arises. Old patterns still attempt to resurface. But they no longer reign.

Walking by the Spirit means:

- Saying no to sin more quickly
- Confessing failure more honestly
- Turning back to Christ more readily
- Growing in discernment and self-control
- Victory is not measured by sinlessness, but by dependence.

Reflection & Discussion

1. Which fruit of the Spirit do you see growing in your life right now?
2. Which areas feel slow or difficult—and why might patience matter there?
3. How does understanding Galatians 5:16 help you respond to ongoing struggle without despair?
4. What does "walking by the Spirit" look like in your daily routines?

Section 3 - The Christian Marriage

Marriage is a covenant designed by God to reflect something far greater than itself—the relationship between Christ and the church.[3]

> "This mystery is profound, and I am saying that it refers to Christ and the church." —Ephesians 5:32

Scripture presents marriage as a lifelong, covenantal union between one man and one woman, established by God for companionship, fruitfulness, and mutual sanctification. Marriage is not a human invention shaped by culture, but a divine institution designed to display gospel realities.

It transforms the self-centered "me" into a unified "we," sharpening individuals to become more like Christ through shared joys, sorrows, and sanctifying challenges.

In marriage, husbands are called to love their wives sacrificially, modeling Christ’s self-giving love for the church. This love is marked not by dominance, but by humility, leadership, and service. Wives are called to respect and support their husbands, joyfully partnering with them in the shared life God has entrusted to them. Both husband and wife are equal in dignity, worth, and value before God.

God uses marriage as a means of sanctification. Through forgiveness, patience, prayer, communication, and moral faithfulness, spouses grow together in Christlikeness. Marriage does not exist to complete a person, but to glorify God by displaying the gospel through covenant love.

Key Reflections in a Believer's Life:

- **Sacrificial Love (Agape):** Moving beyond feelings to actively putting your spouse's needs above your own, mirroring Christ's self-giving love (Ephesians 5:25).
- **Unconditional Commitment:** A steadfast, covenantal bond, not just a contract, reflecting God's enduring faithfulness.

- **Unity & Oneness:** The "one flesh" reality of marriage symbolizes the union between Christ and His Church (Genesis 2:24).
- **Sanctification & Growth:** The marriage serves as a "blacksmith" process, exposing rough edges and, through God's grace, sharpening both spouses to become holier and more Christ-like.
- **Grace & Forgiveness:** Demonstrating God's profound forgiveness and compassion through daily interactions, bearing witness to His mercy.
- **Service & Submission:** Husbands leading with sacrificial headship, and wives responding with godly submission—both willingly submitting to Christ and to one another under God's authority.
- **Glorifying God:** The ultimate purpose shifts from personal fulfillment to magnifying God and displaying His nature to a watching world.

Marriage reflects an upward and outward focus. Living for God's glory (upward) and as a witness to others (outward), rather than inward self-satisfaction.

The marriage covenant also points beyond itself to intimacy with God. As spouses grow in trust, vulnerability, and self-giving love, marital intimacy becomes a living reminder of God's covenant love for His people.

Christian marriage is not about self-fulfillment alone, but about glorifying God through faithful love, forgiveness, and perseverance.

Reflection & Discussion

1. How does the gospel shape expectations within Christian marriage?
2. How can marriage be used by God as a means of spiritual growth?
3. In what ways does marriage expose areas where grace is still needed in your heart?

Section 4 - Parenting in the Lord

God calls parents to nurture their children as a sacred stewardship, not as owners but as caretakers entrusted with lives that ultimately belong to Him.[4]

> "Bring them up in the discipline and instruction of the Lord."
> —Ephesians 6:4

Biblical parenting is rooted in the gospel. Parents are not commanded to save their children, but to raise them to know and love God by reflecting Christ's character and modeling godliness while depending on God for the outcome. Authority in parenting reflects God's character—firm yet compassionate, structured yet loving.

Children learn not only through instruction, but through example. Parents who walk in repentance, humility, forgiveness, and faithfulness demonstrate the reality of new life in Christ. Parenting, like marriage, is one of God's chosen means of sanctification—shaping both children and parents into greater conformity to Christ.

Some Core Principles & Practices For Parenting:

- **View Children as God's Gift:** Recognize they belong to God and are entrusted to you for stewardship, not as possessions to fulfill your dreams.
- **Focus on the Heart:** Aim for deep heart change (desires, beliefs) towards God, not just outward obedience, by addressing root issues.
- **Model Christ:** Live out your faith authentically, showing transformation, repentance, forgiveness, and God's love, so children see the real Jesus.
- **Teach God's Word Diligently:** Integrate faith into daily life, conversations, and times of instruction (Deuteronomy 6:7).
- **Pray Constantly:** Pray for your children and with them, relying on God's power and grace.
- **Discipline with Grace:** Use correction, instruction, and consistent love to guide, not just punish, reflecting God's character.
- **Build Godly Character:** Cultivate virtues like compassion, humility, and kindness, teaching children to value others (Philippians 2:3).
- **Foster Godly Relationships:** Create a home where faith, doubts, hopes, and the Gospel are discussed openly.

What this looks like in Families:

- Families should be reading the Bible, praying together, talking about faith, and church involvement.
- Parents are kind, humble, and honest about their own failings.

- Children will come to know, love, and serve God, reflecting His glory. While parents are called to faithfulness, the work of regeneration belongs to God alone.

It involves prayer, discipline rooted in love, consistent instruction from Scripture, and relying on God's power for guidance and grace, all while delighting in them as God delights in us.

Reflection & Discussion

1. Why is modeling faith as important as teaching it?
2. How can parents depend on God rather than their own strength in raising children?

Section 5 - Singleness and Contentment

Scripture affirms singleness not as a deficiency, but as a distinct calling with unique opportunities for devotion to the Lord.[5]

"Each has his own gift from God." —1 Corinthians 7:7

Singleness is not a waiting room for real life, nor is marriage a spiritual promotion. Both are gifts of God, suited to different seasons and purposes. Those who are single are called to live faithfully, wholeheartedly, and purposefully for Christ in their present state.

While Scripture acknowledges natural desires and varied seasons of life (Matthew 19:12), it consistently encourages believers to embrace their assigned situation with joy—trusting

God for fulfillment and serving Him faithfully, whether single or married. Neither state defines spiritual worth; both are arenas for obedience, joy, and growth.

Contentment flows from knowing that identity, fulfillment, and worth are found in Christ—not in marital status. Whether single or married, believers are fully united to Christ and fully welcomed into the family of God.

Singleness, rightly understood, offers particular freedom: freedom to serve without divided attention, freedom to invest deeply in the church and community, and freedom to pursue Christ with undistracted devotion. This calling is not lesser—it is purposeful.

Finding Contentment in Christ

- **Contentment in Any Situation**
  Contentment is learned through resting in Christ, not by demanding specific earthly circumstances. Paul's contentment was rooted in Christ's sufficiency, not in changing conditions (Philippians 4:11–12).
- **God's Sufficiency**
  Marriage cannot ultimately satisfy the soul—only God can. Whether single or married, believers are called to hold earthly relationships lightly and Christ supremely (1 Corinthians 7:31).
- **A Choice Rooted in Trust**
  Contentment involves actively trusting God's wisdom and goodness, seeking His kingdom first, and believing that He withholds no good thing from His children (Matthew 6:33).

- **Embracing the Present Season**
  Singleness is not wasted time. It is a season to steward energy, gifts, and opportunities for God's purposes with intention and joy (1 Corinthians 7:33–34).
- **A Life of Gratitude**
  Thanksgiving guards the heart from bitterness and comparison, anchoring joy in God's faithfulness rather than unmet expectations (1 Thessalonians 5:18).
- **Honest Dependence on Christ**
  Scripture does not deny loneliness. It invites believers to bring those longings to Christ, who meets His people with compassion, presence, and sustaining grace (Matthew 6:25–26).

Singleness, like marriage, is not an end in itself. It is a context in which new-creation life is lived out—where Christ shapes desires, redirects affections, and displays His sufficiency. In every season, the believer's calling is the same: to belong fully to Christ and to live for His glory.

Reflection & Discussion

1. How does the gospel redefine fulfillment apart from marital status?
2. What challenges or opportunities does singleness present for Christian growth?

Section 6 - Vocation and Daily Faithfulness

Living for God's Glory in Ordinary Life

The Christian life is not confined to church gatherings or spiritual activities alone. Scripture teaches that every area of life

– work, family, service, and daily responsibility – is a sphere in which God is honored and His grace is displayed. A believer's vocation and daily faithfulness are expressions of loyalty to God, lived out through trustworthy, diligent, and loving obedience in ordinary tasks.[6]

> "Whatever you do, do all to the glory of God."
> —1 Corinthians 10:31

Vocation is not limited to pastoral ministry or overtly religious service. God calls His people to glorify Him through diligence, integrity, excellence, and faithfulness in all lawful work—whether paid or unpaid, public or unseen. Ordinary tasks become acts of worship when they are done in faith, dependence on God, and love for others.

Christian obedience in vocation does not aim at self-promotion or personal identity. It flows from gratitude for salvation and a desire to honor Christ. Work becomes a means through which believers reflect God's order, creativity, faithfulness, and goodness in the world.

Faithfulness in Daily Life

Faithful living is marked not by visibility but by consistency. God is honored when His people live with integrity and devotion in both great responsibilities and small details.

• Spiritual Disciplines
Daily prayer, Scripture intake, and fellowship keep believers grounded in God's truth and dependent on His grace.

• Reliability and Integrity
Faithfulness shows itself in keeping commitments, speaking truthfully, and living transparently before others.

• Handling Trials with Trust
Believers remain obedient even when circumstances are difficult, trusting God's promises rather than reacting in bitterness or despair.

• Mercy and Compassion
Christian faith expresses itself through love—meeting physical and spiritual needs and serving others as an extension of Christ's care.

• Transformed Attitudes
Daily faithfulness includes turning away from anger, self-focus, and resentment, and choosing compassion, humility, preparation, and Christ-centered thinking.

Faithfulness in Vocation (Work & Calling)

God uses work as a place where His people learn perseverance, humility, and service.

• Excellence and Honesty
Arriving prepared, completing tasks diligently, and handling time and resources with integrity honors God.

• Service to Others
Believers serve coworkers, customers, and communities as though serving Christ Himself.

"Truly, I say to you… you did it to Me." —Matthew 25:40

• **Stewardship**
Jobs, skills, opportunities, and resources are entrusted by God and are to be managed for His purposes, not merely personal advancement.

• **Humility and Dependence**

Faithful work recognizes God as the ultimate provider and seeks His glory above recognition or reward.

All true faithfulness is sustained by grace. It is not driven by self-effort alone but produced by the Spirit's work within the believer. Faithfulness itself is a fruit of the Spirit (Galatians 5:22), flowing from a heart transformed by the gospel.

Reflection & Discussion

1. How does viewing work and daily responsibilities as worship change motivation and perspective?
2. In what ordinary areas of life is God calling you to greater faithfulness and trust?

Section 7 - Living Faithfully in a Fallen Culture

Believers are called to live **in the world without belonging to it.**[7]

> "Do not be conformed to this world but be transformed by the renewal of your mind."
> —Romans 12:2

Christian faithfulness requires clarity, conviction, and grace in a culture increasingly hostile—or indifferent—to biblical truth. Scripture calls believers to stand firm, speak truth in love, endure hardship, and shine as lights in a darkened world.

Cultural engagement flows not from fear or anger, but from confidence in God's sovereignty. Christ will build His church. The Christian's task is not to preserve power, but to remain faithful – living visibly transformed lives that bear witness to the truth of the gospel.

Cultural engagement does not flow from fear, anger, or a desire to control outcomes, but from confidence in God's sovereignty. Christ will build His church. The Christian's task is not to preserve cultural power, but to remain faithful—living visibly transformed lives that bear witness to the truth of the gospel.

The Christian life flows from salvation and displays it. Empowered by the Spirit and grounded in union with Christ, believers walk in repentance, holiness, love, and obedience—not to earn God's favor, but because they already have it.

Renewing the Mind in a Confused World

To live faithfully in a fallen culture, believers must actively renew their minds with Scripture, allowing God's truth—not cultural narratives—to shape their thinking, values, and conduct. Christians are called to live as **salt and light**, engaging the world with humility and courage, obedience and compassion, truth and love—relying on the Holy Spirit for wisdom and strength.

Below are several dominant cultural narratives believers must recognize and resist:

• **Individualism and Personal Expression**
The belief that personal autonomy and self-expression are ultimate values often undermines biblical community and accountability. Scripture emphasizes life together in Christ, mutual responsibility, and sacrificial love within the body of believers.

• **Feelings as Final Authority**
Modern culture often treats emotions as the final measure of truth and authenticity. While emotions matter, Scripture teaches they must be shaped and governed by God's wisdom. Truth does not originate within us—it is revealed by God.

• **Materialism and Worldly Success**
The message that worth and happiness come from wealth, achievement, or status stands in direct contrast to the gospel, which declares that true joy is found in knowing God, loving others, and living with eternal hope.

• Truth as Subjective
The prevailing idea that truth is personal or relative challenges the Bible's claim to objective, revealed truth. Scripture presents God's Word as historically reliable, morally authoritative, and universally binding.

• The Primacy of Human Freedom
Culture often elevates personal freedom above all else, even redefining identity and morality. Scripture teaches that humans are made in God's image and that true freedom is found not in self-rule, but in joyful submission to God's design.

• Apathy Toward Religion
Secular culture may not openly oppose faith, but often treats it as irrelevant. Believers must resist spiritual drift by keeping Christ central, refusing to compromise biblical truth for cultural acceptance.

• Political Idolatry
There is a temptation to confuse political allegiance with spiritual faithfulness. Scripture reminds believers that they are citizens of a greater kingdom. Earthly systems may be engaged thoughtfully but ultimately never trusted.

Living faithfully means holding truth without arrogance, conviction without cruelty, and hope without despair. The believer's confidence rests not in cultural approval or political outcomes, but in Christ Himself.

Reflection & Discussion

1. Which cultural narratives do you find most challenging to resist, and why?
2. How can believers engage culture with both truth and grace without compromise?
3. What does it look like to renew your mind daily in a world that pressures conformity?

Chapter Summary

Those whom God saves; He transforms. The Christian life flows from a new identity in Christ and is sustained by the Holy Spirit. Whether in marriage, singleness, family, work, or cultural engagement, believers are called to live out the new creation God has made them to be.

Preparing for the Next Chapter

Because the Christian life is not meant to be lived in isolation, Scripture now turns our attention to life together in the body of Christ—the church. In the next session, we will explore God's design for the local church, including worship, fellowship, membership, leadership, and mutual care.

> "So then you are no longer strangers and aliens, but fellow citizens with the saints and members of the household of God."
> —Ephesians 2:19

Chapter 8 Endnotes

1. Scripture consistently grounds Christian obedience in identity, not merit (Col. 3:1–4; Eph. 2:10).
2. The Holy Spirit is the active agent of sanctification and growth in the Christian life (Gal. 5:16–25).
3. Marriage is designed to reflect Christ's relationship with the church (Eph. 5:22–33).
4. Parenting is a stewardship requiring discipline, instruction, and dependence on God (Eph. 6:1–4).
5. Singleness and marriage are both honored callings in Scripture (1 Cor. 7:7–8).
6. All vocation may glorify God when done in faith and obedience (Col. 3:23–24).
7. Christians are called to faithful witness in a fallen world while trusting God's sovereign plan (Matt. 5:14–16; Rom. 12:2).

CHAPTER 9

WORSHIP, FELLOWSHIP, AND LIFE IN THE CHURCH
THE HOUSEHOLD OF GOD

Chapter Overview

Salvation does not merely reconcile individuals to God—it gathers them into a redeemed community. From Genesis to Revelation, God's saving work has always formed a people who belong to Him and to one another—the church.[1]

Christianity is never a private faith lived in isolation. From the moment of conversion, believers are placed into a living community designed by God for worship, growth, and witness.

> "You are no longer strangers and aliens, but you are fellow citizens with the saints and members of the household of God."
> —Ephesians 2:19

To belong to Christ is to belong to His church. The Christian life is never meant to be lived in isolation, but in committed fellowship with God's people under Christ's lordship.

Section 1 - The Church Defined

The church is the people of God called out of the world by grace and united to Jesus Christ by faith. Scripture uses the word church (Greek: ekklesia, meaning "called-out assembly") to describe a gathered people—those whom God has called out of darkness into the light of His salvation.

The church is not a building, denomination, or program. It is the redeemed people of God.

> "You are the body of Christ and individually members of it."
> —1 Corinthians 12:27

As the "body of Christ," the Church is His visible representation on earth, with believers as its members. Jesus is the ultimate leader and source of life for the Church (Ephesians 1:22).

Scripture speaks of the church in two related ways:

- **The universal church** — all true believers across all times and places
- **The local church** — a visible, covenantal gathering of believers in a specific place

The universal church reminds believers that salvation transcends culture, geography, and history. The New Testament emphasizes the local church as God's ordained context for worship, discipleship, accountability, and mission. It is within the local church that believers gather, where their faith is lived out, nurtured, and displayed through real relationships.

Reflection & Discussion

1. How does Scripture's definition of the church challenge common cultural views?
2. Why is the local church essential to Christian growth and faithfulness?

Section 2 - Christ the Head of the Church

The church belongs to Christ. He established it, purchased it with His blood, and rules it by His Word and Spirit.[2]

> "I will build My church, and the gates of hell shall not prevail against it."
> —Matthew 16:18

Christ alone is the head of the church. No pastor, council, tradition, or authority stands above Him. His leadership is exercised through Scripture, not human decree, and through the Spirit, not coercive power. The church thrives not by innovation or control, but by faithful submission to Christ.

> "He is the head of the body, the church."
> —Colossians 1:18

Christ governs His church through His Word and by His Spirit. All authority in the church flows from Him, not from human leaders, traditions, or preferences.

Because Christ is the head:

- The church submits to Scripture.
- The church depends on grace, not human wisdom.
- The church reflects Christ's character.

Christ is the mind of the Church, meaning He provides perfect direction. You are called to listen to Him through Scripture and prayer for wisdom, not just human ideas.

The Church exists under Christ's leadership to reflect His character and carry out His purposes in the world.

- **Submit Your Will:** You yield your personal desires to His will, as a servant to a Master.
- **Love the Church:** You see other believers as part of your own spiritual body and are called to love and encourage them.
- **Obey God First:** You prioritize obedience to Christ, even when it's difficult or goes against popular opinion.
- **Grow in Him:** You constantly seek to grow closer to Him, allowing Him to lead you into all truth and love.

This truth guards the church from abuse, division, and drift. Leadership exists to serve under Christ's authority, not to replace it.

Reflection & Discussion

1. What does it mean practically for Christ to rule His church?
2. How does Christ's headship bring security and direction to church life?

Section 3 - The Purpose of the Church

God has ordained the church to serve several distinct yet unified purposes within His redemptive plan.[3]

These purposes are not optional additions to Christian life; they are central to how God forms, sustains, and displays His people in the world.

Worship

The church exists to glorify God. When believers gather, they do so to exalt the Lord through prayer, Scripture, song, and the proclamation of His Word.

> "Ascribe to the LORD the glory due His name."
> —Psalm 96:8

Corporate worship reorients the hearts of God's people away from self and toward the greatness of God. It reminds believers who God is and who they are before Him.

Edification

The church is the primary context in which believers are taught, encouraged, corrected, and built up in the faith. God has given the church teachers and shepherds to equip the saints for ministry and to help believers grow toward spiritual maturity.

> "Let us consider how to stir up one another to love and good works."
> —Hebrews 10:24

Through sound teaching, exhortation, and mutual encouragement, the church strengthens believers to live faithfully in a fallen world (Ephesians 4:11–16).

Fellowship

Life together in Christ provides mutual care, accountability, and shared joy. Believers are not called to walk alone, but to bear one another's burdens and grow together in grace.

> "They devoted themselves to the apostles' teaching and the fellowship, to the breaking of bread and the prayers."
> —Acts 2:42

Biblical fellowship is more than social connection; it is a shared life rooted in the gospel, marked by love, sacrifice, and perseverance (Acts 2:42; 1 John 3:11).

Witness

The church bears public testimony to the gospel through both word and deed. As God's redeemed people, believers are sent into the world to proclaim Christ and make disciples.

> "You are the light of the world."
> —Matthew 5:14

The church's witness flows naturally from worship, discipleship, and fellowship. A transformed people display the transforming power of the gospel to a watching world (Matthew 28:19–20).

These purposes are not competing priorities, but inseparable expressions of the church's calling. Worship fuels discipleship. Fellowship strengthens endurance. Teaching anchors the mission. When one of these purposes is isolated from the others, the church becomes distorted.

The church exists not for entertainment, convenience, or self-preservation, but to glorify God by displaying the life-changing power of the gospel.

Reflection & Discussion

1. Which purposes of the church are most emphasized—or neglected—today?
2. How does understanding the church's purpose shape your participation in church life?

Section 4 - The Means of Grace in the Church

God has appointed ordinary means through which He nourishes His people spiritually within the church. These means do not save, but they serve the saved.

The **Word of God** stands at the center. Through preaching and teaching, God's Word instructs, reproves, corrects, and trains believers in righteousness. Reading, hearing, and preaching the Bible is fundamental for faith and understanding.[4]

> "Faith comes from hearing, and hearing through the word of Christ."
> —Romans 10:17

Prayer expresses dependence on God and aligns the church with His will. It is the means by which believers communicate with God, seeking forgiveness, strength, and guidance.

Fellowship provides encouragement, accountability, and spiritual care.

The ordinances—baptism and the Lord's Supper—serve as visible signs that proclaim the gospel and reinforce faith, without conferring saving grace apart from Christ Himself.[8]

Baptism Is an Outward Sign of an Inward Reality
At its core, **baptism is an outward expression of an inward transformation** that happens when a person puts their faith in Jesus Christ.

It's the public declaration of a personal decision to follow Him —not the cause of salvation, but the confession of it.

> "Therefore, if anyone is in Christ, he is a new creation. The old has passed away; behold, the new has come."
> —2 Corinthians 5:17

Baptism shows that transformation in visible form — **dying to the old life and rising to new life in Christ.**

Baptism Symbolizes Union with Christ in His Death and Resurrection

> "Do you not know that all of us who have been baptized into Christ Jesus were baptized into his death? We were buried therefore with him by baptism into death, in order that, just as Christ was raised from the dead by the glory of the Father, we too might walk in newness of life."
> — Romans 6:3–4

So, baptism **illustrates the gospel**:

- Going **under the water** = dying and being buried with Christ
- Coming **up from the water** = being raised with Him to new life

It's a **living sermon** of salvation — your story told in water.

Baptism Is a Step of Obedience to Jesus Christ
After His resurrection, Jesus commanded His disciples:

> "Go therefore and make disciples of all nations, **baptizing them** in the name of the Father and of the Son and of the Holy Spirit."
> — Matthew 28:19

This shows that baptism is not optional. It's the **first act of obedience** for a new believer.

It's how a person says publicly,
"I believe in Jesus, I belong to Him, and I will follow Him."

Baptism Marks Entrance into the Covenant Community — the Body of Christ

Baptism is not just individual — it's communal.

> "For in one Spirit we were all **baptized into one body**—Jews or Greeks, slaves or free—and all were made to drink of one Spirit."
> — 1 Corinthians 12:13

It's the **visible initiation** into the family of faith, just as communion is the **ongoing fellowship** within that family.

Baptism Is a Public Profession of Faith and Repentance

When Peter preached at Pentecost, he called for two responses:

> "Repent and **be baptized** every one of you in the name of Jesus Christ for the forgiveness of your sins."
> — Acts 2:38

Baptism follows repentance — it's the believer's public statement that:

- "I have turned from sin."
- "I have trusted in Christ."
- "I now live for Him."

In the New Testament, belief and baptism were closely linked — people were baptized *immediately* after trusting Christ (**Acts 8:36–38, Acts 16:31–33**).

Baptism and Communion: The Biblical Order

In Scripture, baptism is consistently seen as the **first act of obedience** after believing the gospel.

> "So those who received his word were baptized, and there were added that day about three thousand souls. And they devoted themselves to the apostles' teaching and the fellowship, to the breaking of bread and the prayers."
> —Acts 2:41–42 (ESV)

Notice the sequence: **believed → baptized → fellowship/communion**.

Thus, baptism functions as the **public declaration** of faith—an outward sign that a person belongs to Christ and His body. Communion, on the other hand, is a **continuing act** of fellowship with that body.

The Meaning of Communion

Communion (the Lord's Supper) is a covenant meal shared among those who have:

- Been **united with Christ** (through faith and symbolized by baptism),
- Are **walking in fellowship** with Him and His church,
- And are **examining themselves** rightly before partaking (**1 Corinthians 11:27–29**).

The Core Idea in 1 Corinthians 10:16–17

> "The cup of blessing that we bless, is it not a participation in the blood of Christ? The bread that we break, is it not a participation in the body of Christ? Because there is one bread, we who are many are one body, for we all partake of the one bread."
> —1 Corinthians 10:16–17

These verses show two central truths:

1. Communion is **a participation (*koinōnia*) in Christ Himself.**
2. Communion expresses **the unity of believers who already make up Christ's body.**

So, when you take communion, you are:

- Publicly identifying with Christ's death and resurrection, and
- Publicly declaring your belonging to His body, the Church.

That unity presupposes a recognized, covenantal entry into the body—something baptism publicly demonstrates.

So, when Paul says in **1 Cor. 10:16–17** that communion is a "participation" in Christ's body, he's referring to a fellowship that presupposes one has **already entered that body**—which baptism publicly demonstrates.

Through these ordinary means, God does extraordinary work—strengthening faith, granting assurance, correcting error, and drawing believers closer to Christ.

The church is not sustained by innovation, but by faithful devotion to what God has ordained.

Reflection & Discussion

1. Why does God use ordinary means to produce spiritual growth?
2. How do the Word and ordinances strengthen faith over time?
3. How do baptism and communion help guard assurance without replacing faith?

Section 5 - Membership and Commitment

The New Testament assumes that believers belong to identifiable local congregations. While Scripture does not prescribe a single model of church membership, it clearly calls believers to committed participation in a local body.[5]

> "You are the body of Christ and individually members of it."
> —1 Corinthians 12:27

This participation is not merely informal or occasional, but relational, accountable, and enduring.

Commitment to a local church provides structure for discipleship, accountability, and mutual care. It guards against isolation and consumer Christianity by calling believers to live out their faith in a covenant relationship with others.

Biblical membership is not about status or control, but about shared responsibility—loving one another, submitting to godly leadership, and laboring together for the gospel.

It's a commitment to "one-anothering" in the New Testament sense—encouraging, serving, bearing burdens, and holding one another accountable (Romans 12:10; Galatians 6:2; Hebrews 3:13).

It's a formal, mutual pledge to a specific group of believers, like a spiritual family. Membership is a commitment or promise to love, serve, encourage, and gently correct fellow members, allowing them to care for you.
"Membership means I pledge to faithfully participate, use my gifts to help others, and be accountable to my brothers and sisters in Christ here."

Membership isn't about getting something; it's about giving your life to God's people for His glory, following the example of the early church found in the New Testament.
Membership reflects the reality that Christianity is a shared life, not an individual pursuit.

Reflection & Discussion

1. Why is commitment essential for healthy church life?
2. How does accountability serve as a gift rather than a burden?

Section 6 - Leadership and Authority in the Church

Christ shepherds His church through qualified leaders whom He gifts and appoints for the care of His people.[6]

"Shepherd the flock of God that is among you." —1 Peter 5:2

Church leadership exists to serve, not to dominate. Leaders are called to teach sound doctrine, guard the church from error, and model Christlike character. Their authority is **ministerial, not absolute**—derived from Scripture, exercised by example, and always accountable to Christ.

Biblical authority in the church flows downward from Christ, not upward from human power. Leaders do not rule by coercion or control, but by faithful teaching, humble service, and sacrificial care for souls. Their task is not to replace Christ's authority, but to steward it faithfully for the good of His people.

Leadership in the church is therefore **servant leadership**, patterned after Christ Himself:

"The Son of Man came not to be served but to serve." —Mark 10:45

This kind of leadership guides through influence rather than force, conviction rather than pressure, and truth rather than manipulation. It seeks the spiritual maturity, unity, and faithfulness of the body—not personal recognition or control.

Healthy church leadership nurtures growth by:

- proclaiming and defending God's Word
- equipping believers for ministry
- caring for souls through shepherding and prayer
- modeling repentance, humility, and obedience

Biblical leadership is marked by:

- **Humility and service**
- **Faithfulness to Scripture**
- **Genuine care for souls**
- **Accountability before God**

Authority in the church is never an end in itself. It exists under Christ and for the benefit of His people, promoting peace, order, protection, and spiritual growth within the body.

When leadership is rightly exercised, the church is strengthened, guarded against error, and equipped to grow in love and truth.

Reflection & Discussion

1. What distinguishes biblical leadership from worldly leadership?
2. How does godly leadership serve as a protection and blessing to the church?

Section 7 - Unity and Love in the Church

The church is marked by unity grounded in truth and sustained by love.[7]

Christian unity is the visible, relational oneness among diverse believers that reflects the perfect unity of the Triune God and serves as a powerful testimony to the world of Christ's redeeming love.

> "By this all people will know that you are My disciples, if you have love for one another."
> —John 13:35

Christian unity is not created by shared personalities, preferences, or backgrounds. It is created by shared life in Christ. Just as the Father, Son, and Holy Spirit exist in perfect unity, so God's redeemed people are called to live together in unity—diverse yet one, distinct yet bound together in Christ.

Unity is **not uniformity**, nor is it achieved by minimizing doctrine or avoiding truth. True unity flows from shared submission to Christ and His Word. It is rooted in the gospel and expressed through love—patience with one another, forgiveness when wronged, humility in disagreement, and sacrificial service for the good of others.

Scripture describes the church as one body with many members, each uniquely gifted and necessary.

> "...that there may be no division in the body, but that the members may have the same care for one another."
> —1 Corinthians 12:25

Each believer contributes to the health of the whole. When one member suffers, all suffer. When one rejoices, all rejoice. Unity is preserved not by sameness, but by mutual care and shared purpose.

Because believers are still being sanctified, conflict will arise. The gospel does not ignore this reality—it addresses it. Unity is maintained not by pretending differences do not exist, but by responding to conflict with repentance, grace, and reconciliation. The same gospel that reconciled sinners to God also reconciles believers to one another.

The church, therefore, is not a gathering of perfected people, but a community shaped by grace. Life together in the church is not an optional supplement to salvation—it is one of its intended fruits. Through worship, discipleship, fellowship, and mission, God displays His glory and preserves His people until the end.

Reflection & Discussion

1. Why is unity essential to the church's witness in the world?
2. What most commonly threatens unity in the church, and how does the gospel address those threats?

Chapter Summary

God does not save isolated individuals—He saves a people. The church is Christ's body, purchased by His blood, governed by His Word, sustained by His grace, and called to display His love and truth together. Life in the church is not optional; it is central to God's design for Christian growth, perseverance, and witness.

Preparing for the Next Chapter

In the next chapter, we will turn our attention to life within the Christian home—examining marriage, parenting, singleness, and daily faithfulness as expressions of life in Christ.

> "Christ loved the church and gave Himself up for her."
> —Ephesians 5:25

Chapter 9 Endnotes

1. The church consists of all who are united to Christ and gathered by the Spirit (Col. 1:18; Eph. 2:19–22).
2. Christ alone is the head and authority of the church (Matt. 16:18; Eph. 1:22–23).
3. Scripture identifies worship, edification, fellowship, and witness as central purposes of the church (Acts 2:42–47).
4. The Word of God stands at the center of the church's life and growth (2 Tim. 3:16–17; Rom. 10:17).
5. Local church commitment provides structure for discipleship and accountability (1 Cor. 12:12–27).
6. Church leadership serves under Christ's authority for the good of His people (1 Pet. 5:1–4).
7. Christian unity is grounded in truth and expressed through love (John 13:34–35; Eph. 4:1–6).
8. Baptism and the Lord's Supper are Christ's ordinances for the church, serving as visible signs that proclaim the gospel and strengthen faith, without imparting saving grace apart from Christ (Matt. 28:19; Acts 2:41–42; 1 Cor. 10:16–17; 1 Cor. 11:27–29).

CHAPTER 10

THE CHRISTIAN HOME AND DAILY DISCIPLINE

FAITH LIVED WHERE LIFE IS LIVED

Chapter Overview

Salvation does not remove believers from ordinary life—it transforms it; it bears fruit in daily life.

God's design is not that faith be confined to church gatherings or spiritual conversations, but that it shapes the home, daily routines, and unseen moments of life.

Christian maturity is not measured by public visibility, but by private faithfulness.

Those who have been united to Christ by faith are called to live out that union in the ordinary rhythms of home, work, relationships, and personal discipline. The gospel reshapes not only what believers believe, but how they live, even in the most routine and unseen places.

> "As for me and my house, we will serve the LORD."
> —Joshua 24:15

This chapter focuses on **how faith is lived out daily**, especially within the home—the primary environment where character is formed, obedience is tested, and Christlikeness is revealed.

Section 1 - The Christian Home as a Place of Discipleship

From the beginning, God designed the home as a primary place of spiritual formation. Long before formal institutions or public instruction, the household served as the setting where faith was taught, modeled, and passed on from one generation to the next.[1]

> "And these words that I command you today shall be on your heart. You shall teach them diligently to your children, and shall talk of them when you sit in your house, and when you walk by the way, and when you lie down, and when you rise."
> —Deuteronomy 6:6-7

Grace-Shaped Homes

Christian homes are not defined by perfection, but by grace. They are shaped by repentance, forgiveness, patience, and ongoing dependence upon Christ. Parents and children alike grow through ordinary faithfulness—confessing sin, extending forgiveness, correcting with love, and returning again and again to the mercy of God.

The gospel becomes visible in the home as forgiveness replaces resentment, humility overcomes pride, patience tempers frustration, and love governs discipline. A Christ-centered home does not conceal weakness—it brings weakness to the cross. Faith lived at home is not about maintaining appearances, but about continually turning to Christ together.

Ordered Relationships

Scripture presents the family as an ordered yet loving structure in which every member bears dignity, responsibility, and value.

- Husbands are called to sacrificial leadership patterned after Christ (Ephesians 5:25).
- Wives are called to intelligent, willing partnership (Ephesians 5:22–24).
- Children are instructed to honor and obey their parents (Ephesians 6:1–3).
- Parents are charged with guiding without discouraging, discipling with love and patience (Ephesians 6:4).

These relationships do not save—but they reflect the transforming power of salvation already given. The home becomes one of the clearest places where the fruit of the gospel is displayed.

The Home as a Mission Field

Faithfulness in the home equips believers for faithfulness beyond it. God uses ordinary family life to cultivate patience, responsibility, compassion, and trust—virtues essential for service in the church and witness in the world.

The Christian home becomes a place where:

- God's Word is honored.
- Grace is practiced.
- Repentance is modeled.
- Love is made visible.

Much of this faithfulness is unseen by others, but deeply formative. God often does His quietest and most enduring work within the walls of the home.

Reflection & Discussion

1. Why is the home such a powerful place for spiritual formation?
2. What challenges make faithful living at home especially difficult?
3. How does grace—not perfection—shape a Christ-centered household?

Section 2 - Personal Discipleship and Daily Discipline

Spiritual growth does not occur automatically, nor does it replace dependence on grace. Scripture calls believers to disciplined faith as a response to God's mercy.[2]

Personal discipleship and daily discipline in the believer's life involve modeling Christ, intentional teaching, and integrating faith into everyday rhythms. This includes habits such as regular Bible reading, prayer, conversations about faith, serving others, and applying biblical truth to real-life challenges. The aim is heart transformation, not mere behavior modification.

> "Train yourself for godliness."
> —1 Timothy 4:7

Daily personal discipleship includes practices such as:

- **Repentance and confession — moment by moment.** When convicted by the Holy Spirit, believers are called to respond quickly—confessing sin, turning from it, and moving forward in grace.
- **Regular intake of Scripture — consistency is key.** Growth is nourished through steady exposure to God's Word. Even small portions, read faithfully, shape the mind and heart over time.
- **Prayer and dependence on the Spirit.** Prayer is not merely scheduled communication, but a posture of daily reliance—seeking guidance, confessing sin, expressing gratitude, and walking in the Spirit's power.
- **Guarding the heart and mind.** Believers are called to filter influences, set wise boundaries, and fill their inner life with truth—protecting the heart from bitterness, lust, pride, and distraction.
- **Resisting sin and putting on Christlike virtues.** The Christian life involves active resistance to sinful desires and intentional pursuit of humility, love, obedience, and righteousness—by the Spirit's strength.
- **Faithful stewardship of time, resources, and responsibilities.** Recognizing that all things belong to God, believers manage their time, talents, and treasure with wisdom, generosity, and purpose—seeking God's glory rather than personal gain.

These disciplines do not earn God's favor. They are means by which believers grow in maturity, shaped by the Spirit through obedience rooted in grace.

Reflection & Discussion

1. What does "training yourself for godliness" look like in your real, everyday life right now?
2. Which spiritual disciplines come most naturally to you—and which feel most difficult or neglected? Why do you think that is?
3. How do you usually respond when the Holy Spirit brings conviction—do you resist it, delay it, or respond quickly?
4. What helps you stay consistent with Scripture and prayer when life feels busy, exhausting, or distracting?
5. How do you guard your heart and mind in a culture that constantly pulls your attention in other directions?
6. Where do you most often feel tempted to rely on self-effort instead of daily dependence on God's grace?
7. How can daily disciplines be practiced as acts of love and trust rather than duty or pressure?
8. Who has modeled faithful daily discipleship for you—and what have you learned from their example?

Section 3 - Christian Marriage

Marriage is designed by God to reflect Christ's relationship with His church. **Scripture presents marriage as a covenantal union between one man and one woman**, not merely a social arrangement or personal contract, but a sacred covenant through which God works sanctification, faithfulness, and love.[3]

> "This mystery is profound, and I am saying that it refers to Christ and the church."
> —Ephesians 5:32

Christian marriage is not centered on self-fulfillment but on the display of the gospel. God uses marriage to shape hearts, expose sin, and cultivate Christlike love through daily acts of forgiveness, patience, humility, and sacrifice.

Husbands and wives are called to live out the gospel together:

- Husbands are called to love their wives sacrificially, modeling Christ's self-giving love for the church (Ephesians 5:25).
- Wives are called to respect and support their husbands, partnering joyfully in God's design (Ephesians 5:22–24).
- Both are equal in dignity and worth before God, united as one flesh, and accountable to Christ.

Marriage moves believers from a self-focused *"me"* to a covenantal *"we."* It is a daily calling to serve rather than demand, to forgive rather than keep record, and to love in ways that reflect Christ's grace to a watching world.

What Christ-Centered Marriage Looks Like Day by Day

A Christ-centered marriage is not defined by perfection, but by direction—two sinners walking together toward Christ.

Practical Daily Expressions:

- **Spiritual Disciplines**
  Praying together, reading Scripture, worshiping, and serving in the life of the church.
- **Grace-Filled Communication**
  Speaking truth in love, listening humbly, confessing sin, and resolving conflict without bitterness.
- **Sacrificial Service**
  Choosing to serve one another in ordinary tasks, expressing gratitude, and meeting needs without keeping score.
- **Faithful Intimacy**
  Protecting emotional and physical intimacy as a gift from God, cultivated through trust, time, and tenderness.
- **Humility and Repentance**
  Yielding personal preferences, forgiving quickly, and returning often to the cross.

Marriage does not exist to complete a person, but to glorify God by displaying covenant love shaped by the gospel. When lived faithfully, it becomes one of God's most powerful instruments of sanctification.

Reflection & Discussion

1. How does marriage expose both sin and grace in everyday life?
2. In what ways can marriage serve as a means of spiritual growth and sanctification?
3. What does a Christ-centered marriage look like in ordinary routines—not just on Sundays?

4. How can husbands and wives support one another's walk with Christ more intentionally?
5. When communication breaks down, what promises of God can couples cling to?

Section 4 - Parenting and the Discipleship of Children

Parents are entrusted with the stewardship of lives created for eternity. Parenting is not merely about behavior management or success in this world, but about faithfully pointing children toward the God who gives life.[4]

> "Bring them up in the discipline and instruction of the Lord." —Ephesians 6:4

Biblical parenting is rooted in the gospel. Parents are not called to save their children—that work belongs to God alone—but they are called to raise them in an environment where Christ is known, honored, and trusted. Faithful parenting involves Scripture instruction, loving discipline, humility, prayer, patience, and persistent gospel witness.

Children are shaped not only by what they are taught, but by what they observe. The spiritual atmosphere of the home matters. When repentance is normal, grace is visible, forgiveness is practiced, and Christ is honored, children see the gospel lived out before them.

God's Design for Parental Authority

Scripture calls parents to a form of authority that reflects God's own character—firm yet compassionate, structured yet loving.

"Do not provoke your children to anger" (the negative command)

- Avoid harshness, inconsistency, favoritism, or unrealistic expectations.
- Guard against discipline that flows from frustration rather than love.

"Bring them up" (the positive command)

- **Gentle Nurture:** Treat children with patience, affection, and care.
- **Love with Authority:** Discipline that corrects without crushing.
- **Humility:** Acknowledge your own sin and need for grace.

Gospel-shaped parenting combines truth and love—clear boundaries with deep compassion.

Discipline and Instruction in the Lord

Paul uses two complementary ideas to describe Christian parenting:

Discipline (Training / Nurture)
This refers to shaping character through consistent guidance,

correction, and example. Discipline is not merely punishment; it is loving formation aimed at wisdom and maturity.

Instruction (Teaching / Admonition)
This involves intentionally teaching God's truth—through conversation, Scripture, prayer, and daily life. Parents are called to speak about God naturally and consistently, not only in moments of crisis.

Practical rhythms include:

- Regular prayer with and for children
- Reading and discussing Scripture together
- Talking about faith in everyday moments
- Modeling repentance, forgiveness, and dependence on God

Parents can disciple children most powerfully by being disciples themselves.

Faithfulness Without Fear

Parenting is a long work, often marked by uncertainty and prayerful waiting. Scripture reminds parents that obedience matters more than outcomes.

The goal is not perfect children or flawless parents, but homes oriented toward Christ—homes where the gospel is visible, spoken, and trusted.

Reflection & Discussion

1. What do your children (or those you influence) learn most clearly about God by watching your daily life?

2. How does understanding that God—not parents—gives new life bring both humility and peace?
3. Where might discipline or instruction drift toward control rather than gospel-shaped care?
4. If your home had a "mission statement," what would it say—and does it reflect Christ?
5. What small, realistic changes could help make faith more visible in everyday family life?

Section 5 - Singleness and Devotion to Christ

Scripture honors singleness not as a deficiency, but as a gift—one that provides unique opportunities for devotion to the Lord.[5]

> "The unmarried man is anxious about the things of the Lord, how to please the Lord."
> —1 Corinthians 7:32

Singleness is not a waiting room for life to begin, nor is marriage a spiritual promotion. Like marriage, singleness is a God-given context in which faithfulness, obedience, and devotion to Christ are lived out. Scripture presents singleness as a meaningful calling, not a lesser one.

Those who are single are fully complete in Christ and fully integrated into the family of God. Identity, worth, and fulfillment are never measured by marital status, but by union with Christ. The single believer lacks nothing spiritually and stands on equal ground with every other member of Christ's body.

Singleness offers distinct opportunities for focused devotion, service, hospitality, and ministry. Without the unique responsibilities of marriage, single believers often have greater flexibility to invest deeply in prayer, Scripture, discipleship, and the needs of others within the church. This season—whether temporary or lifelong—is not wasted time, but purposeful time entrusted by God.

Marks of Faithful Singleness

- **Undivided Focus**
  Singleness allows for concentrated attention on spiritual growth, prayer, and holiness without divided obligations (1 Corinthians 7:32–34).
- **Availability for Service**
  Greater flexibility often enables single believers to serve readily—through discipleship, hospitality, missions, and meeting practical needs within the church family.
- **Investment in Spiritual Family**
  Singleness creates space for deep relationships within the body of Christ—serving as spiritual brothers, sisters, mothers, and fathers in the household of faith.
- **Contentment in Christ**
  True satisfaction flows from Christ, not circumstances. Singleness testifies that Jesus alone is sufficient to meet the deepest longings of the heart.
- **Wise Stewardship**
  Time, energy, and resources can be intentionally stewarded for kingdom purposes—generosity, service, and gospel advance.
- **Purposeful Living**

> Faithfulness is not postponed until marriage. God calls single believers to live fruitfully, obediently, and joyfully in the present season He has given.

Contentment is not passive resignation, but active trust in God's wisdom and goodness. Whether single or married, believers are called to live fully devoted lives—seeking Christ first and trusting Him to order every season according to His perfect will.

Reflection & Discussion

1. How does finding identity in Christ reshape the way singleness is viewed in the church and in personal life?
2. What unique opportunities does singleness provide for spiritual growth and service?
3. How can single believers invest meaningfully in the life of the church as a spiritual family?
4. What helps guard against loneliness while cultivating healthy contentment in Christ?
5. How can single believers pursue relationships wisely without making marriage an idol?

Section 6 - Faithfulness in Vocation and Daily Life

The Christian life is not confined to gathered worship or overtly "spiritual" moments. It is lived out in work, responsibility, perseverance, and obedience in the ordinary rhythms of daily life. Scripture calls believers to faithfulness—not flashiness, recognition, or visible success.[6]

> "Whatever you do, work heartily, as for the Lord."
> —Colossians 3:23

Vocation—whether paid or unpaid—is one of the primary arenas in which faith is displayed. Work becomes worship when it is offered to God in trust, integrity, diligence, and love.

Faith is not proven only in moments of prayer or proclamation, but in reliability, honesty, patience, and quiet obedience when no one is watching.

Faithfulness does not mean perfection. It means loyal obedience—doing what God calls us to do, trusting Him with the results.

Faithfulness in Vocation (Work and Calling)

God calls His people to reflect His character through their work. Whether a believer is a laborer or a leader, a parent or a professional, a student or a retiree, vocation is a stewardship entrusted by God.

- **Serve with excellence** – Give your best effort, even when unappreciated, remembering that you ultimately serve the Lord, not human employers.

- **Glorify God through integrity** – Speak truthfully, handle resources honestly, and refuse shortcuts that compromise faith.

- **Meet real needs** – Use skills and labor to serve others and contribute to human flourishing, reflecting God's care for creation.

- **Be trustworthy** – Keep commitments, arrive prepared, and act consistently with Christian character, even in small matters.

Work is not a means of self-definition or personal worth, but an opportunity to honor God and love neighbor.

Faithfulness in Daily Life

Beyond formal vocation, faithfulness is practiced in the rhythms of everyday life.

- **Prioritize spiritual disciplines** – Build prayer, Scripture, and fellowship into daily life as foundations, not afterthoughts.
- **Practice steady obedience** – Follow God's commands even when obedience is costly, inconvenient, or unnoticed.
- **Demonstrate steadfast love** – Love family, friends, and neighbors with patience and perseverance, reflecting God's covenant faithfulness.
- **Persevere in ordinary tasks** – Cooking, cleaning, caregiving, budgeting, and routine responsibilities become sacred when done in faith.
- **Live by trust, not outcome** – Leave results in God's hands, believing He is faithful even when efforts seem fruitless.

Faithfulness is not measured by visible success, but by obedience sustained over time. It is the quiet consistency of a life anchored in Christ.

The believer's freedom in Christ does not lead to passivity, but to joyful obedience. Because salvation is secure, faithfulness becomes a grateful response—not an attempt to earn God's favor.

Reflection & Discussion

1. How does viewing your work or daily responsibilities as service to the Lord reshape your motivation?
2. Where are you tempted to disconnect faith from "ordinary" parts of life?
3. What does faithfulness look like for you in unseen or uncelebrated tasks?
4. How does trusting God's faithfulness help you persevere through frustration or weariness?
5. Are there areas where you measure success by results rather than obedience?
6. How does freedom in Christ empower you to live faithfully rather than fearfully?

Section 7 - Living in Light of Eternity

Daily faithfulness is sustained by eternal hope. The Christian life is not lived merely for the present moment, but in light of what is coming. Scripture repeatedly calls believers to lift their eyes beyond temporary circumstances and fix their hearts on eternal realities.[7]

> "Set your minds on things that are above."
> —Colossians 3:2

Believers live as pilgrims—engaged in this world, yet not anchored to it. Earthly success, comfort, recognition, and security are fleeting. The hope of resurrection, final redemption, and eternal fellowship with Christ gives weight and meaning to obedience that often goes unseen and unrewarded in the present age.

To live with an eternal perspective is not to neglect daily responsibilities, but to invest them with lasting purpose. Ordinary acts of faithfulness—serving others, stewarding resources, resisting sin, enduring suffering—become expressions of hope rooted in what God has promised to complete.
Scripture teaches that this life is preparation for glory.

What Living in Light of Eternity Looks Like

- **Kingdom Focus**
  Prioritizing God's purposes over worldly success, wealth, or comfort—recognizing that earthly life is brief, but eternity is unending.
- **Christ-Centered Living**
  Seeking to glorify Christ in every sphere of life, finding motivation not in personal gain, but in love for the One who gave Himself for us.
- **Purposeful Stewardship**
  Using time, talents, and resources wisely for eternal impact—laying up treasure in heaven rather than accumulating what cannot last.

- **Evangelism and Discipleship**
  Living with awareness of eternal destinies, compelled by love to share the gospel and invest in others for the sake of Christ.
- **Eternal Relationships**
  Valuing unity, forgiveness, and love within the church—building bonds that will outlast this life.
- **Peace and Resilience**
  Resting in God's promises during trials, knowing that suffering is temporary and glory is certain.
- **Holiness and Sacrifice**
  Choosing righteousness even when it costs, trusting that obedience now leads to joy forever.
- **Watchful Faithfulness**
  Living alert, faithful, and ready—serving Christ with expectation of His return.

To live in light of eternity is to see this life as a training ground for the life to come—making choices today shaped by the certainty of resurrection and the promise of everlasting joy with Christ.

Reflection & Discussion

1. Where are you currently setting your mind—on "things above" or on earthly concerns? What makes an eternal focus difficult?
2. If someone observed your life for a week, would they conclude that your hope is rooted in resurrection and eternity?
3. How do your beliefs about heaven and hell influence your daily priorities and decisions?

4. How does an eternal perspective help you navigate suffering, loss, failure, or uncertainty?
5. What practices help you cultivate gratitude and hope rooted in eternal realities?

Final Exhortation: From Knowledge to Response

The journey from death to life does not end in doctrine alone. Truth calls for response—not self-reform, but trust; not earning, but faith.

Salvation rests entirely on Christ's finished work. Yet the gospel that saves also summons. God calls His people to live faithfully—not to secure salvation, but because salvation has already been freely given in Christ.

If you are in Christ, you are called to live where God has placed you—resting in grace, walking in obedience, and trusting His promises until the day you see Him face to face.

If you are not in Christ, the invitation still stands:

> "Come to Me, all who labor and are heavy laden, and I will give you rest."
> —Matthew 11:28

Chapter 10 Endnotes

1. Scripture presents the home as a primary context for discipleship (Deut. 6:6–7; Eph. 6:4).
2. Spiritual disciplines function as means of growth, not grounds of salvation (1 Tim. 4:7–8).
3. Marriage reflects Christ's relationship with the church and serves sanctification (Eph. 5:25–32).
4. Parenting emphasizes faithfulness to God's Word and reliance on grace (Prov. 22:6).
5. Singleness is affirmed as a gift for devoted service to Christ (1 Cor. 7:7, 32).
6. Faithful vocation honors God and serves others (Col. 3:23–24).
7. Christian obedience is shaped by eternal hope, not fear or merit (Col. 3:1–4).

CONCLUSION

From Death to Life: A Final Invitation

The story of salvation is the story of God's sovereign grace—His pursuit of sinners, His provision through Christ, and His power to bring the dead to life. From the opening pages of Scripture to the final promises of Revelation, the Bible proclaims one message with unwavering clarity: **God saves sinners through Jesus Christ.**

You have walked through the testimony of Scripture—
the holiness of God,
the fall of humanity,
the seriousness of sin,
the person and work of Christ,
the life-giving power of the Holy Spirit,
the order of salvation,
and the lived expression of new life in the church, the home, and the world.
And now, the question stands before every reader:
What will you do with Jesus Christ?

The gospel is not merely a set of truths to understand.
It is a **Savior to trust**.
It is a **Lord to follow**.
It is a call to turn—from sin, from self, from darkness—and to come to Christ for life.

To conclude this book, let us walk through one of the clearest and most faithful gospel summaries found in Scripture—often called the *Romans Road.* These verses do not replace the gospel message you have already read; they simply gather its truths into a clear and personal invitation.

THE ROMANS ROAD:

God's plan of salvation

Paul's Epistle to the Romans sets forth the gospel with unmatched clarity. In just a few passages, the path from death to life is unmistakably revealed.

1. We Are All Sinners

"For all have sinned and fall short of the glory of God." — Romans 3:23

Every human being stands in the same condition before God. Sin is not merely a failure to live up to personal standards—it is falling short of **God's glory**. No one is righteous by nature. No one meets God's perfect standard. All are accountable to Him.

2. Sin Brings Death

"For the wages of sin is death, but the free gift of God is eternal life in Christ Jesus our Lord."
—Romans 6:23

Sin earns a wage, and that wage is death:

- physical death
- spiritual separation from God
- eternal judgment

But the verse does not end with judgment. God offers something sin never could: **a free gift—eternal life in Christ Jesus our Lord**.

3. Christ Died for Sinners

> "But God shows His love for us in that while we were still sinners, Christ died for us."
> —Romans 5:8

God did not wait for sinners to improve themselves. He did not require reform before rescue. In love, Christ came to us. At the cross, He bore sin, absorbed judgment, and satisfied divine justice. The wrath sinners deserved fell on Him. The righteousness sinners lacked is offered to them in Him.

4. Salvation Requires a Response

> "If you confess with your mouth that Jesus is Lord and believe in your heart that God raised Him from the dead, you will be saved." —Romans 10:9

Salvation is not earned by works—but it does call for a response.
That response includes:

- confessing Jesus as Lord
- believing in His resurrection
- trusting Him fully and personally

Faith is not mere agreement with facts. It is a wholehearted reliance on Christ Himself.

5. God's Promise Is Sure

> "For everyone who calls on the name of the Lord will be saved."
> —Romans 10:13

God's promise does not rest on the strength of the call, but on the faithfulness of the Savior.
No sin is too great.
No past is too dark.
No heart is beyond the reach of grace.

Everyone who calls on Jesus Christ in repentance and faith will be saved.

APPENDIX A — THE GOSPEL - FROM DEATH TO LIFE IN CHRIST

The gospel is the good news of what God has done to save sinners through Jesus Christ. It is not advice, instruction, or moral improvement. It is an announcement of divine rescue accomplished by God and received by faith.

1. God Is Holy and Sovereign

God is the eternal Creator of all things. He is perfectly holy, righteous, and just. He rules over all creation with absolute authority and perfect wisdom. Nothing stands outside His will, and nothing compromises His holiness.

Because God is holy, sin cannot be overlooked. Because He is just, guilt must be judged. Because He is sovereign, salvation must come from Him.

2. Humanity Is Sinful and Accountable

Humanity was created in God's image but fell into sin through Adam's disobedience. As a result, all people are born sinful by nature, guilty before God, spiritually dead, and unable to save themselves.

Sin is not merely wrongdoing—it is rebellion against God. Its consequences are spiritual death, physical death, and eternal judgment. No moral effort, religious practice, or sincerity can remove guilt or restore fellowship with God.

> "All have sinned and fall short of the glory of God."
> —Romans 3:23

3. Christ Is the Only Savior

God's solution to sin is not self-improvement but salvation through His Son. Jesus Christ is the eternal Son of God who became fully man while remaining fully God. He lived a sinless life, obeyed God's law perfectly, and came with a single purpose—to save sinners.

At the cross, Jesus bore the punishment sin deserved. He absorbed God's righteous wrath in the place of His people. His death was substitutionary, sufficient, and final. On the third day, He rose from the dead, defeating sin and death. He ascended into heaven and reigns as Savior, Mediator, and King.

> "There is salvation in no one else."
> —Acts 4:12

4. Salvation Is by Grace Alone

Salvation is not earned, deserved, or achieved. It is a free gift of God's grace. Sinners contribute nothing but their need. God saves by mercy, not by human effort.

Grace is not assistance—it is rescue.
Grace is not cooperation—it is resurrection.

> "But God… made us alive together with Christ."
> —Ephesians 2:4–5

5. Salvation Is Received Through Repentance and Faith

Although salvation is entirely God's work, it is personally received through repentance and faith. Repentance is turning from sin and self. Faith is trusting wholly in Jesus Christ—His person and His finished work.

Faith is not a meritorious work; it is reliance on Christ alone. Those who trust in Him are forgiven, justified, adopted as God's children, and given eternal life.

> "If you confess with your mouth that Jesus is Lord and believe in your heart that God raised Him from the dead, you will be saved."
> —Romans 10:9

6. God's Promise Is Certain

God's invitation is sincere, and His promise is sure. Everyone who comes to Christ in repentance and faith will be saved. No sinner is beyond grace. No past is too dark. No guilt is too great.

> "For everyone who calls on the name of the Lord will be saved."
> —Romans 10:13

A Final Word

Salvation is not found in religion, morality, or self-effort. It is found in a Person—Jesus Christ. To reject Him is to remain in sin and judgment. To trust Him is to pass from death to life.

The gospel does not ask what you can do for God.
It declares what God has done for you in Christ.

A Personal Word to the Reader

If you have read this book and recognize yourself in its pages—if you see now that you had religion without redemption, knowledge without new life, or belief without repentance—do not harden your heart. Christ is not reluctant to save. He does not turn away those who come to Him.
He receives sinners gladly.

If God could take a man who lived a divided life—confident in religious activity yet enslaved to sin—and bring him from death to life, **He can do the same for you**.

That is the gospel.
That is the hope of these pages.
That is why this book exists.

FROM DEATH TO LIFE

The gospel is not merely information. **It is an invitation.** Jesus Christ stands ready to save all who come to Him in repentance and faith.

> "Come to Me, all who labor and are heavy laden, and I will give you rest."
> —Matthew 11:28

May God use these pages to awaken your heart, strengthen your faith, grant true assurance, and draw you into the joy of knowing Jesus Christ.
To Him be all the glory.

APPENDIX B — HOW TO USE THIS AS A STUDY GUIDE

For Leaders and Participants

This study guide is designed to help individuals and groups grow in a clear, biblical understanding of salvation and the Christian life. It is not intended to be rushed, mastered, or completed as a checklist, but to be engaged prayerfully, thoughtfully, and honestly.

Whether you are using this guide personally or in a group setting, the goal is the same:

to listen carefully to God's Word, respond humbly to His truth, and grow in assurance, obedience, and love for Christ.

For Participants

1. Come Ready to Listen

This study is grounded in Scripture. Each session invites you to hear what God has revealed—not to defend yourself, impress others, or compare experiences. Come ready to listen with humility and openness.

You are not expected to have all the answers. Growth begins with honesty before God.

2. Read Slowly and Thoughtfully

Each chapter is designed to be read carefully. Do not feel pressured to rush through material. Take time to:

- read Scripture attentively,
- reflect on the teaching,
- consider how God's Word speaks to your life.

Some truths may challenge long-held assumptions. Allow Scripture—not emotion or habit—to shape your understanding.

3. Engage the Reflection & Discussion Questions Honestly

The questions at the end of each section are not tests. They are invitations:

- to examine your heart,
- to articulate what you are learning,
- to apply truth personally.

Honest reflection is often where God does His deepest work.

4. Remember the Goal Is Clarity, Not Confusion

If questions arise, that is not a failure—it is often a sign of growth. Salvation is not meant to be mysterious or uncertain. God desires His people to know Him, trust Him, and walk in assurance.

Bring your questions to Scripture, prayer, and discussion rather than suppressing them.

5. Be Patient with Yourself

Spiritual growth is a process. Some sessions may feel clear and encouraging; others may be uncomfortable or convicting. Do not measure progress by emotion, but by increased clarity, humility, and dependence on Christ.

For Group Leaders

1. Your Role Is to Guide or Facilitate Discussion

This guide is not designed to showcase the leader's knowledge. In truth, you need no deep theological background to lead a group through this study. Your role is to:

- facilitate Scripture-centered discussion,
- encourage honest participation,
- keep the focus on God's Word rather than personal opinion.

Resist the urge to answer every question immediately. Allow Scripture to speak and participants to think.

2. Create a Safe and Respectful Environment

Many sections touch on deeply personal matters—assurance, sin, repentance, family life, and faith struggles. Encourage:

- confidentiality,
- respect,
- patience with one another.

Avoid pressuring participants to share beyond what they are comfortable expressing.

3. Keep the Discussion Grounded in Scripture

When discussion drifts toward speculation, debate, or personal experience as authority, gently bring it back to Scripture. The power of this study lies in God's Word, not in human insight.

Encourage participants to answer questions with biblical truth rather than feelings alone.

4. Allow Time for Prayer

Prayer is not an add-on to the study—it is an essential response. Consider opening and closing each session with prayer, asking God to:

- grant understanding,
- convict where needed,
- give assurance,
- and strengthen faith.

Prayer reminds the group that transformation is God's work.

5. Be Sensitive to Where People Are

Groups may include:

- new believers,

- long-time church members,
- those struggling with assurance,
- those still seeking clarity about salvation.

Avoid assumptions. Let the gospel speak freshly to every heart, including your own.

Final Encouragement

This study guide is not about producing perfect Christians, but about pointing imperfect people to a perfect Savior.

Salvation is not earned through participation in a study—it is received by grace through faith in Jesus Christ. This guide exists to clarify that truth, deepen understanding, and strengthen assurance.

May God use these sessions to:

awaken hearts,

ground faith in truth,

strengthen families and churches,

and draw His people into deeper joy and obedience.

From death to life—
This is the work of Christ.

BIBLIOGRAPHY

Primary Source

- **The Holy Bible**, English Standard Version (ESV). Crossway.

Theology & Doctrine

- Grudem, Wayne. *Systematic Theology.* Zondervan.
- Sproul, R.C. *What Is Reformed Theology?* Baker Books.
- Sproul, R.C. *The Holiness of God.* Tyndale House.
- Berkhof, Louis. *Systematic Theology.* Eerdmans.
- Calvin, John. *Institutes of the Christian Religion.* Translated by Henry Beveridge. Hendrickson.

Christology & Salvation

- Athanasius. *On the Incarnation.* Popular Patristics Series.
- MacArthur, John. *The Gospel According to Jesus.* Zondervan.
- Murray, John. *Redemption Accomplished and Applied.* Eerdmans.
- Packer, J.I. *Knowing God.* InterVarsity Press.
- Horton, Michael. *Putting Amazing Back into Grace.* Zondervan.

Biblical Interpretation

- Beale, G.K. *A New Testament Biblical Theology.* Baker Academic.
- Motyer, J.A. *Look to the Rock: An Old Testament Background to Our Understanding of Christ.* Kregel.
- Carson, D.A. *Exegetical Fallacies.* Baker Academic.

Christian Living & Sanctification

- Bridges, Jerry. *The Discipline of Grace.* NavPress.
- Bonhoeffer, Dietrich. *The Cost of Discipleship.* Touchstone.
- Ferguson, Sinclair. *The Holy Spirit.* InterVarsity Press.
- Ferguson, Sinclair. *Devoted to God.* Banner of Truth.

About the Author:

John A. Woolwine is a follower of Jesus Christ whose life stands as a testimony of God's transforming grace. Though raised in church and actively involved in ministry for many years, he later came to realize that religious activity is no substitute for regenerative faith. Through the convicting and life-giving work of the Holy Spirit, God brought him from spiritual death to new life in Christ.

John writes not as a theologian detached from experience, but as a man deeply shaped by Scripture, repentance, and grace. His passion is to help others understand the true message of salvation, avoid false assurance, and grow in joyful obedience and confidence in Christ.

He lives with his wife, Edna, and is grateful for their children and grandchildren, for whom this study guide was prayerfully written.

www.ingramcontent.com/pod-product-compliance
Ingram Content Group UK Ltd.
Pitfield, Milton Keynes, MK11 3LW, UK
UKHW062308290726
14090UKWH00018B/953